UP PERISCOPE

Up Periscope

By DAVID MASTERS

DIAL PRESS　:　:　:　NEW YORK

Yonder bright star, which glorifies the night,
Revealed to Drake the way of destiny,
And Nelson, aided by its steadfast light,
Made his immortal plans for victory.
England awakes again. Her seamen flout
The foe. Eternal beams blaze up on high.
Though tyrants put the lights of Europe out,
One star still lights a beacon in the sky.
Lurking like Fate, the British submarines
Rend the dark silence with their sullen roar,
Attacking the foeman's ships, piercing their screens,
Hurling the wreckage to the ocean floor.
Calmly the sea-breed put once more to sea
To cleanse the world and keep the seaways free.

D.M.

CONTENTS

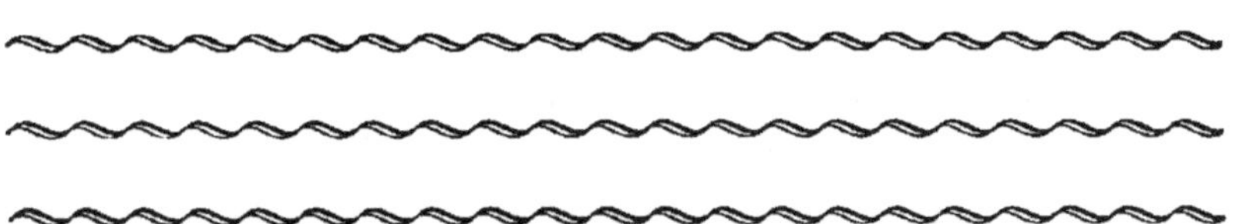

PREFACE

ONLY when Germany is vanquished and all the documents are available for the study of the historian will it be possible to give a full account of the activities of the British submarine flotillas in this war. That they have struck hard blows at the navies of Germany and Italy and Japan is well known; their blows at the merchant fleets of the enemy have been equally damaging. British submarines have in fact destroyed so many Axis ships that the shipping problem can be no less acute to the enemy than to the Allies, but whereas the Allies can look forward to vast fleets of new merchant ships from the shipways of the United States, the Axis powers have no such source of supply to save them.

Not without reason have the British flotillas which operate so brilliantly in the Mediterranean come to be feared, for their torpedoes and shells have wiped out whole convoys—big and small tankers, fine liners converted into troopships, merchant steamers and sailing ships with escort vessels of various kinds make up the fleets which have set out from enemy ports never to return. In European waters the British flotillas have sunk large numbers of enemy ships of all types, and the following pages describe some of the outstanding actions and experiences of British submarines since the war began.

The Royal Navy has won a reputation as the silent service, and this silence is probably even more marked in the submarine service than in other branches. The fog of secrecy which envelops the operations of surface ships is intensified when the submarines operate. The British submarine service is in truth the secret service of the sea.

The eyes of the Admiralty are reconnaissance aircraft of the Royal Air Force which fly high overhead peering down on the waters and harbours of the enemy coasts. But the submarines are more than this—they are the eyes and ears. They see and hear everything that is going on within range. Where the pilots of the Royal Air Force fly over the coasts and harbours to take their photographs and depart, the submarines lurk patiently for days, watching when conditions are right and visibility is good, and listening all the time, night and day, whether visibility is good or bad, hearing ships in many cases long before they can see them.

Ordinary mortals sometimes marvel at the acute sense of hearing developed by the blind, yet the blind man's ears are deaf when compared with the hydro-phone. Since the London-born scientist David E. Hughes invented the microphone which magnified sounds to an enormous degree and was scoffed at by other British scientists when he clearly demonstrated the first wireless waves before Marconi began to work on the subject at all—the United States was less sceptical about the genius of Hughes and rewarded his talents with a huge fortune—the microphone has been developed into the hydrophone which can pick up sounds under water.

The hull of a submerged submarine actually catches the sound waves and acts like a giant hydro-phone. One of the first men to discover this was Simon Lake, the American inventor who did so much to develop the inefficient and dangerous early sub-marine into the modern deadly weapon of war. Long ago he wrote in the *Century Magazine*: "It is surpris-ing how accurately the human ear can detect sound under water. I first discovered in my experiments in Hampton Roads, in 1897, that when the machinery was shut down in the submarine, I could distinguish the approach of surface vessels from considerable distances by simply resting a stick against the plating of a submarine and putting the other end to my ear."

Quite unknowingly, Simon Lake varied the experi-ment of the famous French physician Laennac who invented the stethoscope that has proved invaluable -in diagnosing tuberculosis by the sounds of the lungs. Laennac, who remembered a boyish game in which the scratch of a pin at one end of a beam was heard clearly if the ear were placed at the other end of a beam, eventually invented a small wooden trumpet or tube which was the original stethoscope. The long tube used by inspectors to trace leaks in a water pipe is a giant form of the invention.

"The steel hull of the vessel became a great sound-receiver, and the stick carried the sound waves to the ear," continued Simon Lake. "This did not give a sense of direction, so I devised a rotary receiver which could be rotated on top of the hull to pick up the direction of the sound. Shortly afterward Mr. Munday of Boston introduced his submarine signal and receiving apparatus, which gives a very correct indication of the direction of the sound. Now the Fessenden oscillator improves on that to the extent that conversations may be carried on under water for a considerable distance. Not only can you detect the direction of the sound, but a little experience with the receiver gives a good idea as to distance. Every ship has sounds peculiar to itself, the smash of the paddle-wheels, the slow, but deep pound of the bearings in large, powerfully engined ships, and the high-speed machinery of the destroyer can all be distinguished by the operator at the receiver. Without any sound-receiving device, while in a submarine resting on the bottom with all machinery stopped, I have heard even the whirr of the machinery in a Whitehead torpedo nearly a mile away."

This is no less true to-day than when the American

inventor wrote it. But now the human ears have been touched with a new wonder that has enormously increased their range. Upon the hydrophone operator, listening intently to the sounds which flow to his ears from the sea around him, may depend the success of an attack on a ship or the escape of the submarine from the surface hunters. The lives of the crew may depend upon how he interprets the sounds he hears, and his interpretation must rest on his technical training and experience. He must be able to detect the differences in the sounds of motors and engines. He must note all their variations to tell whether they are speeding up or slowing down. The remarkable powers of the hydrophone have so impressed submarine crews that on occasions when British submarines have been sorely hunted the men have taken off their boots so that they could move about without making the slightest noise. At such times their lives depended on their silence. They knew that the least sound might bring about their destruction.

As may be expected, the submarine crews are the pick of the Navy, for this highly-specialized service offers fine opportunities to the old dauntless spirit which animated Drake and Grenville and which still survives in our finest young men of to-day. To be a member of a submarine crew is a mark of distinction: it connotes intelligence, keenness and physical fitness above the average. The men are trained to become specialists, and their rates of pay are higher than those ruling in surface ships. Every man on board knows his work and does it instantly. They practise together until they become welded into a crew with perfect confidence in each other and in their captain. When on duty each performs his part in the series of mechanical operations which take a submarine safely below the surface and bring her up again. There must be no mistakes. An oversight by one may lead to the death of all. To eliminate errors there is an elaborate system of visual signals for controlling the operation of the boat, while all verbal orders are automatically repeated back to ensure accuracy.

If the crews run any additional risk, they show no indication of it in their bearing. Just before Christmas, 1941, two mothers with their sons in naval uniform were shown in to see a medical friend of mine. He had brought both sailors into the world and their mothers wanted him to see them before they went back from leave.

"What are you doing?" the doctor inquired.

"We're in submarines," was the response.

"A bit dangerous, isn't it?" inquired the doctor in his gentle way.

The young men laughed. "The safest job in the Navy," they asserted and meant it.

Most submarine men will probably agree. They are enthusiasts for their particular branch of the Navy and in their eyes nothing can compare with it.

Submarine crews lead a topsy-turvy life. They turn night into day. This is easy to understand. Their boat relies upon the power from electric batteries to propel it beneath the surface because electric motors do not consume the life-giving air. A submarine must strike without being seen, so during the day it patrols beneath the surface at periscope depth to keep a watch for enemy ships. By the end of the day a good deal of the current has been consumed and it becomes necessary to recharge batteries. This can be done only while the submarine is on the surface and it entails the use of the main engines which are run on oil fuel. Clutches enable the propeller shafts to be disconnected from the main engines which can then be connected up with the motors that serve as dynamos to recharge the batteries. Normally the boat charges on one engine while it travels along on the other, and only when a submarine captain is pressed very hard will he stop his boat to recharge on both engines, because if the enemy comes upon him when stopped, he is caught at a disadvantage.

As the important work of the boat must be done at night, the crew take their main meal between 1 a.m. and 2 a.m. while the submarine is on the surface and they have supper just before they dive for the day patrol. They adapt themselves to these conditions without much trouble, and they are able to revert to normal conditions during their spell ashore with comparative ease.

Their food is of the best, mostly canned. The day to day diet is arranged before the submarine leaves base, and by keeping to the daily menus, which are scientifically drawn up, the crews escape the monotony of the meals of olden days and maintain their fitness despite lack of exercise. At the beginning of the war experiments were made to provide the crews with bread which remained eatable and appetizing from the beginning to the end of patrols lasting several weeks. This was accomplished by sealing the loaves in a special waxed wrapping paper which kept the bread fresh so long as the wrapping was unbroken. In some of the big submarines the cook bakes bread every day, but on the smaller boats this is not possible, but whether the bread be wrapped or freshly baked, the usual biscuits always find their place in the stores and some submariners still prefer them to bread.

The men are unable to smoke when submerged, so it is the custom to take sweets with them on patrol and they may be seen going about their jobs sucking sweets like so many boys. In more than one desperate hunt, these sweets have proved a great solace to the men.

Contrary to popular opinion, a submarine moves at no great speed under water. On the surface she runs on her main Diesel engines which may propel her sufficiently fast to overtake the average merchant ship. When she dives she changes over to her electric motors which propel her normally at an easy walking pace. She can be speeded up if necessary, but a running man could still outpace her when she is going at full speed under water. Her batteries are quickly exhausted at high speed and exhausted batteries make her helpless under attack, unable to move below the surface at all; consequently the skilful captain always uses the power in his batteries in the most miserly manner. He aims always to have sufficient power in hand to allow him to steal away if attacked —which is the reason why he is so desperately keen to recharge his batteries every night. A full charge in the batteries may save the ship and crew, so the experienced captain seldom goes at full speed under the sea for more than a few minutes when it is essential to work into position to make an attack or to avoid the counterattack from surface craft, after which he usually crawls away at one or two knots.

However incongruous it may seem, there are similarities between a submarine and an airship. One floats in air and the other floats in water. The navigation of both depends upon proper balance, and both possess ballast tanks by which the trim, or balance, of the ship is adjusted. To rise quickly, an airship will jettison ballast in its forward tanks to lighten the nose and enable the engines to drive her up at a steeper angle. To achieve a similar result the submarine will use compressed air to blow some of the water from its forward ballast tanks in order to lighten the bow and at the same time alter the angle of the forward hydroplanes so that the pressure of the water on their undersides will push up the bow as the propellers drive her forward.

Without going too deeply into technicalities, it may be said that a submarine is composed of a giant steel cylinder known as the pressure hull, which is divided into water-tight compartments and built strong enough to withstand the pressure of the sea at the limit to which she is designed to dive. This explains why submariners call a submarine a "tube." On the outside of the pressure hull, in addition to the decks and superstructure, are built the ballast and fuel tanks, with further trimming tanks, known as auxiliaries, and freshwater tanks inside the ship. The ballast tanks are filled by opening the Kingston valves which allow the sea to rush in at an enormous rate, thus decreasing the buoyancy and carrying her under the surface, while compressed air is used to blow the water out of the tanks to bring her up again. The hydroplanes at the bow and stern of the boat help in these diving operations and when a submarine is properly trimmed she rises and dives solely by altering the angles of her hydroplanes.

It is all a question of buoyancy. Taking in too much ballast will drive her too deep, expelling too much will send her to the surface. To keep the submarine balanced between these extremes—maintaining trim, as it is called—demands all the skill of the submarine officer. To maintain the exquisite balance which enables a submarine to proceed steadily along at periscope depth throughout the day is something of a conjuring trick, a technical accomplishment that is not learned in a day. A few gallons too much in the tanks may make the periscope dip below the surface, and a few gallons too little may drive the submarine to the top. If the submarine is too near the surface, the captain may have to lie down flat in the control room to use the periscope just as the eyepiece emerges from the periscope well, at other times he may have to crouch or kneel and only when the boat is maintaining a perfect periscope depth may he stand up to look through the periscope in comfort.

It is far simpler to maintain trim in some areas than in others. It depends upon the density of the sea-water, which in turn may vary with the seasons. For instance when the snows melt on the Norwegian mountains, large volumes of fresh water rush down the fiords into the sea. This forms a layer of fresh water flowing like a river in the sea and as it is fed copiously by the melting snows it does not mix readily with the sea-water. Beneath this layer of fresh water will come a layer of sea-water and somewhere below this may be found yet another layer of fresh water.

A submarine needs less ballast to dive in the fresh water than in the denser sea-water, because the fresh water is not so buoyant, as every swimmer knows. A dense layer below the fresh water may make depth-keeping simple, because the submarine will actually float along on the surface of this secondary layer as easily as it floats on the surface of the sea: although the boat is submerged, it is really floating between two layers of different density, with the lower layer of sea-water supporting the submarine like a giant's hand.

Naturally these layers of different densities complicate diving problems for the captain. Some days in certain areas he may find the water so dense that it is difficult to dive at all, and not until he has taken in tons of ballast in excess of normal can he get down. At other times the density may decrease and he finds he can reach the required depth with less than the usual amount of ballast. These variations and layers while they add to his difficulties may sometimes simplify his navigation and there is at least one authentic case of a clever captain who used a layer to save his ship from destruction.

British submarines vary in size from 600 tons up to the big ocean-going boats of roughly 1,700 tons and their crews likewise vary from about thirty to over fifty. The largest submarines can remain at sea for many weeks, during which they can steam thousands of miles without refuelling—although a submarine travels upon the surface on Diesel oil engines, to the submariner she still "steams."

During the patrols the crew never take off their clothes, and the majority do not shave from the time they leave their depot ship until they return. For weeks these keen young seamen live in the closest possible contact in a submarine so crammed with torpedoes and shells and machinery and scientific miracles that even an aircraft cannot compare with it for complexity. The control room is so packed with pipes and dials and wheels and valves that the sight of them sets the mind in a whirl.

PREFACE

One man who entered a control room for the first time just looked round and gasped: "I should never understand it!"

"Oh, yes, you would," said the captain quietly in a voice that inspired confidence. "It's really quite simple."

And so it was—to him!

In this mighty steel cylinder with its maze of pipes and valves and oil engines and giant batteries and electric motors and pumps and fans, the crew eat and sleep and have their being for long periods in the depths of the sea. Life is adventurous. They never know what is going to happen and they carry on calmly at their posts with a bravery that was not surpassed by Drake when he cut out the Spanish ships from Cadiz nor by the sailors of Grenville in that last immortal fight of the *Revenge*.

Theirs is the true heroic spirit, and after the most hazardous enterprises they return to port with a smile in their eyes and a quip on their lips to prepare cheerfully for the next patrol. When things go right they have little to report, but when things go wrong their resolution and courage flame out so brightly that they will light up the eyes of this great nation a thousand years hence.

In saluting all those who man the submarine flotillas of the Royal Navy, I would like to place on record my thanks to the Admiralty and those officers and men without whose courtesy and help this book could not have been written.

DAVID MASTERS

UP PERISCOPE

In reading the following pages, it must be borne in mind that the success of a submarine depends as much upon the courage and team-work of the crew as upon the decisions and leadership of the captain, and the Author wishes to make it clear that any tribute paid to the captain applies to the whole crew. It must also be pointed out that these actions and adventures are merely representative of many more, equally fine and gallant, which it is impossible at present to describe.

RETURN OF

THE *SPEARFISH*

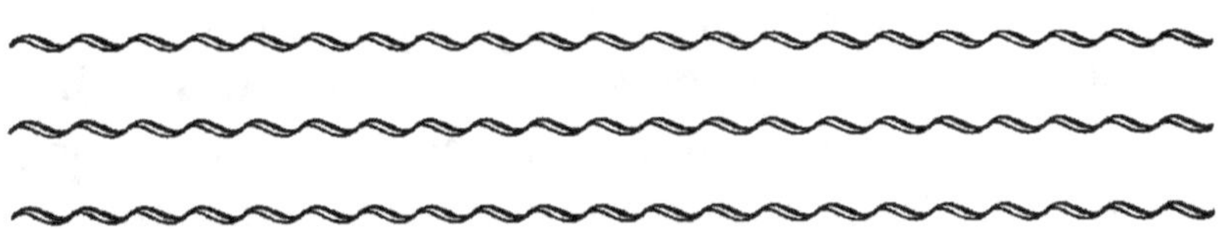

Just after the outbreak of war, Lieutenant J. H. Eaden gave orders to cast off the *Spearfish*, and she slipped quietly away to patrol off the Norwegian coast. In a twenty-knot breeze under a lowering sky, she went steadily on her course. Altering helm to avoid being seen by a merchantman during the night, she dived before dawn to proceed beneath the surface for a couple of hours when, finding the seas empty, she came up to go ahead on her main engines.

By midday the wind and seas were increasing. There was no break in the heavy cloud. Once or twice during the day she changed course or dived to avoid being seen by merchant ships, and by midnight a northerly gale caused her to stagger and roll heavily.

Next morning the seas were running too high for her to proceed at periscope depth, for the waves washing over the periscope made observation impossible, so she steamed on the surface, diving occasionally to dodge any merchantmen she sighted.

By 1 o'clock in the early morning her look-out picked up the beam of a lighthouse on the Norwegian coast. Two hours later a big fishing fleet was sighted, so the Spearfish dived and rested a few hours on the bottom.

Just after 6 a.m. some of her pumps were started to enable her to go up to have a look round. Raising her periscope, her commander saw many trawlers flying the Danish flag with picturesque white hulls and red triangular sails. An artistic eye might have appreciated their pictorial quality, but the quiet eyes of Lieutenant Eaden appraised them from a submariner's point of view. The red sails were like danger signals, warning the *Spearfish* to avoid them—which was exactly what her commander did, for about 8 o'clock in the morning he took her to a lower level.

Ninety minutes later he went up to see what was going on. It was a bit of a shock when he barely missed bumping the keel of a trawler. "I nearly put my after periscope through the bottom," he said afterwards.

Lowering his periscope, he continued on his batteries for a couple of hours before taking her to the bottom where she settled down while her crew rested.

Darkness lay over the seas when the *Spearfish* surfaced. The crew got busy, fans were started to blow out the boat and change the atmosphere, the main engines were set to recharging the batteries, and the navigator manipulated the sextant to fix his position by the stars.

Early on Sunday morning, just before 4 o'clock, the recharging was completed. The crew had eaten their main meal of the day—or night—and the hatch closed as the *Spearfish* slid under the surface to a safe depth. Within half an hour the operator listening at the hydrophones heard a sound.

Sounds coming to the listening ears in a submarine call for instant investigation. They may mean danger, on the other hand they may indicate that a target is somewhere in the vicinity.

Then the keen ears of the listener detected a faint noise which told of a vessel moving ahead.

Other ears, enemy ears, were listening just as intently for the sounds made by the *Spearfish* and enemy hands were waiting to strike her a mortal blow. But the men in the submarine did not know. They could not see. They could only guess.

All doubts about the danger of those strange sounds were resolved in a big explosion which made the *Spearfish* vibrate like a tuning fork. At once her commander took her to the bottom and stopped all machinery.

The *Spearfish* was in a nasty position. She was caught in shallow water which made her very vulnerable, whereas a hundred fathoms would have given her a chance to go deep and steal quietly away.

The best method of escaping the hunter was for the *Spearfish* to lie low and keep absolutely quiet in the hope that the enemy would grow tired and relinquish the chase.

From time to time those peculiar sounds came to the listeners in the submarine. Two hours passed, then Lieutenant Eaden made up his mind to go up to see if anything was in sight.

"Diving stations," he ordered, and instructed the engineer to pump out the main ballast tanks to take them to periscope depth.

Before the pumps had been working five minutes a heavy explosion shook the *Spearfish*. Instantly the commander ordered the pump and all other machinery to be stopped. Even the gyroscope of the gyro-compass upon which the submarine depended ceased to spin.

"See whether there is any damage and report to me," the captain ordered.

"The fuses of the steering motor are blown, sir," said the engineer. This, the only damage, was a simple matter to put right.

Ordering the crew to rest and keep quiet, Lieutenant Eaden waited to see what would happen. His hydrophones were sensitive enough to disclose that two vessels were hunting the *Spearfish*. There were other sounds which told of the hunters methodically sweeping for the submarine.

Just before 8 o'clock the hydrophones picked up the faint sound of a turbine.

Lieutenant Eaden thought things over. They were in grave danger. The enemy who had been hunting them for six hours was stubborn and patient and would not easily be foiled. The hydrophones had told him all they could during the morning. To listen longer would merely increase the nervous tension inside the boat. The crew were behaving normally, yet it was difficult to refrain from listening and wondering what the noises portended, so he ordered the man on listening watch to go off duty.

"I decided on complete silence and remaining stopped on the bottom as the only hope of survival," he said afterwards.

Although the operator no longer listened at the hydrophones, the sounds could not be kept out of the boat. They penetrated the hull for all the crew to hear.

The sound of a depth charge came to them just before 1.30 and five followed within the next three-quarters of an hour. Some were nearer than others, but none was near enough to shake the *Spearfish*.

The incredible coolness of the men stood out when depth charging began. They knew that death might engulf them at any moment, but their sporting instincts were so strong that one of the men suggested a sweepstake to be won by the man who guessed nearest to the time when the next depth charge would explode. The stake was fixed at sixpence a time, to be settled on pay day, and a seaman quietly walked through the boat among the resting men to note their times and names—they had the calm courage to wager their bets on the next charge which might blow them all into eternity as though it were a football pool or a greyhound race!

For a time there was silence. Then just before 3 o'clock the attack started again. Twenty-eight times in an hour the *Spearfish* shook under the force of the explosions.

Again there was silence. The pressure of the air in the submarine began to rise. The men lay about quietly, eating, wondering, dozing, reading, talking in whispers. Then another sound came to their ears, a deadly, ominous sound. They looked at each other. No one spoke. Something slid along the jumping wire —which was rigged, as in all submarines, to enable an obstruction to slide clear of the hull. No one knew what it was, whether it was a grapnel seeking to hook them so that a charge could be sent down to destroy them, or whether it was the wire of a sweep. They listened tensely. No one moved. Something thumped the hull aft. There followed a series of bumps as though a heavy weight suspended on a wire were jerking along just touching the hull.

Then at 5.20 p.m. came an appalling explosion. The hull of the *Spearfish* seemed to close in on the crew as though under a gigantic press and then spring outward again. The lights were shattered. In the darkness the shaken men heard the deadly sounds of spurting water and the sibilant hiss of escaping air.

Swiftly the chief engine-room artificer, S. N. Peel,

sensed that the main motor cooler was damaged. The darkness was absolute, but his skilled fingers barely hesitated as they reached out to shut it off. At the same instant Petty Officer A. P. Blackmore dropped the main motor fuses to cut them out, thus preventing a fire which would quickly have consumed the oxygen in the boat and killed all the crew. Stoker Philpotts lent a hand. Elsewhere two stokers, James W. Smith and Alfred Backers, hearing the high-pressure air escaping, felt round for the valves to isolate the leaks, while stoker James Slade and engine-room artificer Jack M. Smith dealt with other air leaks. Their initiative and courage in the dark were superb.

The voice of Lieutenant Eaden came to them out of the darkness. It was quite normal, as though nothing unusual had happened, a steadying, reassuring voice: "Go quietly to diving stations, use the secondary lighting and investigate damage. Don't make any noise," he ordered.

The men moved to their posts. Soon the emergency lights came on and reports of the damage began to reach the captain.

"The port main motor cooler has burst and the switchboard is covered with water, sir," said F. H. Westnutt the engineer. Hissing air told of serious leaks in the high-pressure air system. Water ran down the ventilator from the main battery, but bad as things seemed, the commander found comfort, for he realized there was no immediate danger of the

Spearfish flooding, that her structure, over which the shipwrights had toiled to make it as strong and perfect as possible, was still intact.

"Fit new light bulbs and sweep up the broken glass," the commander ordered. "And try to stop the leaks of the high-pressure air."

When these things were done, the crew were ordered to rest again. The brain of the captain worked quickly to circumvent his enemies. The Germans may not have known they had scored a hit, in which case, if the men in the *Spearfish* kept very quiet and made no sounds which could be picked up, the hunters might move off. One thing was certain to Lieutenant Eaden: their only chance was to remain silently on the bottom as long as possible.

"The crew behaved magnificently, up to the highest standards of the submarine service," he said, when the ordeal was over.

Another depth charge exploded at a distance, then one near enough to shake the *Spearfish* as though she weighed no more than a few pounds instead of hundreds of tons. At intervals came more explosions until they totalled a dozen, some at a distance, others near enough to rock the submarine. After which things quietened down awhile.

"Issue a tot of rum," ordered the captain at 6 o'clock. They all took it appreciatively. It was eleven hours since the first explosion shook the ship, and during that time they had been under great strain.

The air began to get fouler. To conserve it, the captain ordered all the crew to lie or sit down. His keen eye noticed that several men were breathing more heavily than usual. It was then that Lieutenant D. A. Pirie, who remained as cheery as any man aboard, bethought himself of a bottle of sweets which he possessed. They were passed round and proved a boon to the men.

Within half an hour of receiving their tot of rum, the bow of the ship rose sharply and dropped again. They had no illusions. Even Lieutenant Eaden thought that the enemy had managed to get a wire sweep under their bow, but all they could do was to wait and wonder. Again the bow lifted and fell back with a thud. The men looked at each other. Again and again they underwent this nerve-racking ordeal. Yet the anticipated explosions did not take place. They could not quite understand it.

Later the captain concluded that this action of the bow must have been caused by the *Spearfish* swinging to the tide—and he was probably right, for had the enemy got a heavy sweep under the submarine they would not have survived.

Knowing the increasing foulness of the air would force them to the surface within an hour or two, the captain dealt with his secret papers and ordered a big charge of explosive to be rigged ready to destroy the ship and its secrets.

At 7.20 that evening he called the officers and crew together. "I would first of all like to congratulate you on your steadiness and fine behaviour," he said.

"What I propose to do is to blow the ship to the surface at 20.30. If the enemy is in sight we shall engage them. If not, we shall make our way home."

"Aye, aye, sir!" exclaimed the weary men, smiling approval. When the captain said he would blow the ship to the surface, he merely meant to blow the water out of the main ballast tanks to give her sufficient buoyancy to rise. The men who had been lying about so quietly, thinking and wondering what was going to happen, jumped at the chance of getting at the enemy. If they were to die, at any rate they would die fighting in the true Nelson tradition.

Tired and strained as they were, they got busy, with many a quip among themselves, making preparations to fight the enemy as soon as the *Spearfish* surfaced. Two of the torpedo tubes in the bow were loaded up to give them quick shots at the enemy if the opportunity served, they made ready the shells for the 3-inch gun and saw that the Lewis gun was fully prepared to start blazing away instantly. The exertion in the vitiated air tired them, but they put the final touches to the big charge that would prevent their ship from being captured by the enemy, before donning their life-belts in readiness for anything that might befall.

Half an hour before blowing the tanks, another examination was made of the damage. The hull leaked in several places, fuel and oil tanks were leaking, fractures were found in one of the main engines, the steering gear was out of order, the voice pipes from the control room to the bridge were broken, the internal telegraph system was out of order, a periscope and the wireless were smashed, while the after hydroplane had jammed owing to the shaft being forced out of alignment. Altogether 39 different items of the intricate electrical apparatus and other machinery were damaged by the explosion. Yet neither the captain nor a single member of his crew was dismayed. They were badly knocked about, but they were not knocked out and they still had a fighting chance of survival.

Trying his controls, the captain found the fore hydroplanes worked freely. Then he gave orders to blow the main ballast tanks.

Notwithstanding the efforts made to stop the air leaking from the high-pressure air bottles, the hissing never ceased. The result was that the air pressure inside the submarine had gradually increased until it was much higher than ordinary atmospheric pressure. This extra air was pent up in the submarine just as the air is pent up in a motor tyre, and the commander knew that as soon as he unsealed the conning-tower it would gush out with terrific force, just as the air explodes from a tyre when it is punctured, and there was the risk of his being blown out and injured. This was no imaginary danger, as was proved when Leading Signalman Penny of the *Sturgeon* was blown clean out of the conning-tower right into the sea and was drowned before he could be rescued. All that Lieutenant Eaden had ever learned about submarines and air pressures stood him in good stead. He forgot nothing. His courage and skill and knowledge alike combined to save the *Spearfish* and her crew.

As the tanks emptied and buoyancy returned to the *Spearfish* she rose to the surface.

Selecting his leading signalman, a man weighing 14 stone, the captain instructed him to hang on his legs, to prevent him from being blown out when he opened the hatch. Directly the hatch was unfastened, the pent-up air gushed out with such force that the binoculars round his neck flew up through the opening and were only saved by their strap from going overboard. He gazed around him, and drew the fresh air into his lungs. No enemy was in sight.

Able Seaman E. G. Morey, the gunlayer, whose jests throughout that trying time had done much to hearten his companions, swarmed out ready to fire directly they reached the surface. Breathing the foul air under pressure had affected the crew and two of the men lost consciousness directly they came up, but they soon recovered in the fresh air.

Fortunately the starboard electric motor still operated and on this the *Spearfish* moved slowly forward while the engineers and every man on board strove to repair the damage wrought by the explosion. Pipes were examined and leaky joints tightened. The engineer, F. H. Westnutt, struggled to get the main engines running. Water had got into both and put them out of action, their valves would not work. But fault after fault was traced and rectified until at last after struggling for three hours he got the starboard engine turning. It vibrated a bit, but he had never heard a sweeter sound in his life. Then he turned to tackle the port engine and managed after another fight lasting two hours to clear the water out of it and set it humming. So their chances of escape began to increase.

While the engineers were striving to get the engines going the wireless operator, E. Carlton, was busy repairing the wireless apparatus so that they could signal to base to tell them of their plight. The leaks in the pressure hull prevented the *Spearfish* from diving. When daylight came the crew set about trying to stop these leaks, locating them one by one and plugging them. The worst leak was through a bolt-hole which had to be sealed from the outside by driving a wooden peg into it.

In the morning the wireless operator got his wireless going to warn other British submarines in the area. Then he passed a signal to base.

In due course the signals called the ships of the Royal Navy to see the *Spearfish* safely home. Eight minutes after that signal was received, the first cruiser left port. Such prompt action proved that the Navy was awake. As quickly as possible the destroyers and other forces followed. Never was a submarine provided with a mightier rescue force. If only the German Navy had intervened to try to cut off the *Spearfish,* there would have been one of the big naval battles of the war.

While the great and small ships of the Navy were speeding to rendezvous with the *Spearfish* at midnight, the *Spearfish* was making twelve knots on the surface, moving discreetly, for she was in no shape to court trouble. The tough fibre of the captain is proved by the fact that, although the submarine was in no state to dive, he patrolled during the morning while his crew occupied themselves in plugging the leaks. They were too busy to dwell upon their danger.

That afternoon the look-out sighted two enemy aircraft away to the south, aircraft which had the submarine at their mercy. But Lieutenant Eaden dealt with the danger in masterly fashion. He could not dive, so he took his ship to within 500 yards of some sand dunes which might serve to conceal her, and then manned the Lewis gun and posted two men with rifles to beat off any attack. Fortunately the *Spearfish* was not observed.

An hour later the alarm was repeated as two aircraft were seen, probably the same two enemies flying back again. Once more the luck was with the submarine and although one of the aircraft flew low only two miles away, the *Spearfish*, owing to her position among the sand dunes, escaped notice.

About 8 o'clock that night she set out in the dark to make her rendezvous with the destroyers *Somali* and *Eskimo*. At midnight in the appointed place she picked up her escort, and next morning some of the great ships told off to protect her were sighted, among them the aircraft carrier *Ark Royal*.

That morning two German aircraft shadowed the ships from a distance of 7 miles, but they decided, after the *Glasgow* opened fire on them, that they were a little too close and were content to place a distance of 10 miles between them and the guns of the British Navy. Although the German naval command were fully aware that the British ships were in their waters, they made no attempt to come out and give battle, so the big ships were withdrawn and the *Spearfish* made a safe return.

Less skill on the part of Lieutenant Eaden, a little less luck, and the *Spearfish* might have remained for ever at the bottom of the North Sea.

It was the first remarkable escape of a submarine in the war, and it won the D.S.C. for Lieutenant John Henry Eaden. The Distinguished Service Medal was awarded to Chief Engine-Room Artificer Stanley N. Peel and to Petty Officer Alfred P. Blackmore; while Lieutenant Donald A. Pirie, Frank H. Westnutt, the engineer, Edward C. Carlton, the telegraphist, Jack M. Smith, James W. Smith, Alfred Backers, James Slade and Ernest G. Morey were all mentioned in despatches.

In due course the *Spearfish* was repaired, and Lieutenant-Commander Forbes took her on another adventurous patrol. The things they saw varied between a roving barrage balloon, a mine and a Heinkel seaplane which they avoided by diving. The first excitement came from a Junkers 88 which dropped a bomb about 25 feet away as the *Spearfish* went under and lay low for awhile on the bottom.

In a thick fog which persisted for nearly two days, many enemy aircraft flew unseen overhead and one crashed straight into the sea close by. Judging by these patrols, the captain of the *Spearfish* guessed there might be something on.

Nor was he wrong, for next day his periscope revealed eight vessels sweeping for mines, while three trawlers were on anti-submarine patrol and three destroyers were acting as escort to a large convoy whose smoke smothered the horizon as the ships approached. The *Spearfish* manœuvred to attack, while the *Triton* was also concentrating on the same convoy. One of the destroyers detected the *Triton* and led the others to hunt her. Luck was with the *Triton*, for the destroyers lost her. In seeking her they picked up the sounds of the *Spearfish* and began to attack her desperately, no doubt under the impression that she was the first submarine which they had located.

Moving warily at 5.30 p.m., the *Spearfish* sighted a destroyer coming straight for her. A minute later the depth charges started to explode. They came singly, they came in patterns of four or five, and on three occasions from eight to eleven depth charges were dropped in a geometrical pattern designed to obliterate the *Spearfish*. In sixty-seven minutes, from 5.31 to 6.38 the crew of the *Spearfish* suffered the explosion of 66 charges. Now and again a light was smashed, air-leaks began to develop in the high-pressure bottles with the consequence that the air pressure inside the boat began to rise exactly as on her last patrol. Things quietened for half an hour and blazed up into the closest attack of all, when nine depth charges were dropped in a pattern. They missed, and as silence fell, Lieutenant-Commander Forbes wondered if the Germans had used all their charges and whether they would leave a destroyer to stalk him while the others went off for more.

It was a grim contest, a deadly battle of ears and sounds. Lieutenant-Commander Forbes knew that although sound could betray him to destruction, it could also lead to deliverance. His scientific knowledge told him it must be so. All depended upon his power to create confusing sounds to baffle the listening ears of the enemy and lead them astray.

So he strove to outwit them. To avoid the disaster of being flung to the surface by a depth charge, where the enemy waited to rend him, he considered it essential to gain strong control over the *Spearfish* by using both motors. The risk of the sound betraying him had to be accepted in order to control the submarine in any upsurge of the seas caused by the explosions, for while the *Spearfish* remained invisible the enemy were not sure where to strike.

The hydrophone reports told of the destroyers still in attendance. In vain Lieutenant-Commander Forbes strove to evade them. They trailed him grimly. The situation became so menacing that just after 8 o'clock her captain began to deal with his secret papers and ordered the crew to put on their lifebelts. After preparing to destroy the ship and her vital secrets, he called the crew together to instruct them what to say if they were taken prisoner. He still hoped for the best. At a pinch he might keep under until the morning, then, if the destroyers still remained, he determined to surface and try to torpedo them.

Just before 9 o'clock another sound came to the ears of the hydrophone operator. "Reciprocating engines ahead, sir," he reported.

Lieutenant-Commander Forbes seized a heaven-sent chance, for the sounds of the reciprocating engines might blanket his own sounds and allow him to escape. Calling for full speed ahead, he altered helm and drove on. The hydrophone operator, listening intently, noted with relief that the sounds of first one and then another destroyer died away, until only one destroyer remained in earshot.

By the way the remaining destroyer kept altering course and running in and out, the captain of the *Spearfish* was heartened. She was like a hound which had nearly, but not quite, lost the scent of the fox and was running to and fro trying to pick it up again.

Nevertheless at 9 o'clock the destroyer was still on their trail. A minute or two later a ship with recip-rocating engines passed right over the top of the *Spearfish*. That was their chance of deliverance. Realizing instantly how he could use this new ship to baffle the hunter, the captain altered helm without delay to place this vessel between the *Spearfish* and the destroyer. He aimed to make the reciprocating engines of the ship into a wall of sound behind which the submarine could shelter and escape. The surface ship drowned the sounds of the submarine, as Lieutenant-Commander Forbes planned, and by 11.30 that night the destroyer was shaken off.

The *Spearfish* had been down for twenty hours. The air was very foul, the pressure great. The hunt had lasted six hours and the officers and men were exhausted.

Taking the *Spearfish* to the surface, Lieutenant-Commander Forbes prepared to open the hatch. Knowing well what had happened on the previous patrol, he got his men to fasten him down with ropes in order to save himself from being blown out. In addition he ordered a heavy man to hang on to him. He got the first clip off the hatch, but for a time the second clip defied all his strength. Suddenly the hatch flew back with a clang, so forcibly that part of the counterweight attachment was cracked—counterweights are as necessary to enable the men to open and close the hatch as they are necessary to take the weight of windows to enable them to be opened and closed easily. The damage could not be seen. However it made itself felt later when bad weather broke off the counterweight and flung it into the sea, allowing the hatch to fall upon the head of the captain and injure him.

By that time he had taken revenge for what the *Spearfish* had endured on those two patrols. The first thing he did upon surfacing was to blow the foul air out of the boat and let the men suck the sweet night air into their lungs. It was a tonic to them. Then they prepared for the vital task of recharging the batteries.

Within an hour of coming up, by one of those tricks of Fate, the incomparable fighting spirit of the crew nerved them to fight back and their exhaustion fell from them like a cloak. Just after midnight, when the *Spearfish* was running on the surface at 12 knots, the captain and first lieutenant on the bridge noted the flares falling from aircraft to the north. It was a dark night, but beautifully clear. The first lieutenant looked alertly around. Something seemed to move in the velvety blackness. Staring intently, his keen eyes made out the bow wave of a ship nearly two miles away.

"A ship to starboard, sir," he said.

Thinking it was one of the hunting destroyers, the captain started to turn, while looking through his glasses. That was at 12.30 a.m.

Thirty seconds later he identified a heavy warship and sounded the torpedo alarm. Stopping both engines, he checked the submarine from swinging off her target. The torpedo men, keen to repay, excelled themselves and the torpedoes were ready for firing almost at once. So dark was the night that Lieutenant-Commander Forbes dared not take his eyes off the warship to use the night sight for fear that he might not be able to pick her up again, so he relied upon his own eyes and gave the order to fire a salvo of torpedoes. There were tense seconds of waiting before two explosions told of hits.

The necessity of evading the counterattack made it impossible to identify the warship or learn whether she was sunk, but it is believed to have been the *Admiral Scheer*.

"I am glad the *Spearfish* has had an opportunity of paying off old scores," was the remark of Admiral Sir Max Horton to Lieutenant-Commander Forbes afterwards.

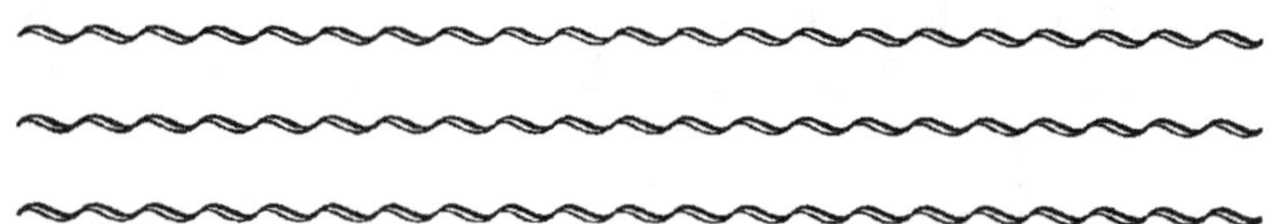

2

AN EPIC PATROL

"This patrol is an epic. It is impossible to speak too highly of the Captain, Officers and Crew of the *Salmon*," was the verdict of Captain P. Ruck-Keene who commanded the flotilla to which the *Salmon* belonged, a verdict endorsed by Rear-Admiral B. C. Watson, who added: "This patrol must surely be unique in the annals of the submarine branch." When high officers who regard things with an impartial eye give this meed of praise, the ordinary man may indeed regard the patrol as exceptional.

It was just before midnight when the captain of the *Salmon*, Lieutenant-Commander Edward Oscar Bickford, slit open a long envelope, which he had been expecting, and read the contents carefully. They were his secret orders to start on an offensive reconnaissance patrol in about twenty-seven hours, at 2.30 a.m. on the following day.

All day the crew of the *Salmon* made their final

preparations. Stores were stowed. Bickford had a final word with his senior, boarded the *Salmon* and precisely at 2.30 a.m. stole away from his base into the darkness of the North Sea. Pushing along on the surface all night, he dived before daybreak and proceeded on his way.

Lieutenant Maurice Fairfax Wykeham-Martyn was on duty next day when he saw through the periscope what appeared to be a box floating on the sea far ahead. Watching it carefully, his acute eye noticed that it did not swing up and down on the waves. "That's not a box," he thought, and steered the *Salmon* up closer to the surface to get a better view.

"Engine noises ahead, sir," reported the hydrophone operator, which confirmed the suspicions of the first lieutenant, whose eye was at the periscope, that it was a U-boat painted green.

The captain, who was called, studied her eagerly. "She's outward bound on passage to her patrol area," he decided, and asked at once for full speed, for he was a long way off the course of the enemy, who was jogging along on the surface oblivious of danger. There was a considerable lop on the waves that sunny afternoon.

Working out the distance and speed of the enemy, the captain ordered a salvo of torpedoes to be prepared.

At length when he had brought the *Salmon* to within range of the enemy he gave orders to fire.

With his eye at the periscope, he saw the torpedoes

follow each other in succession toward the target. One torpedo which failed to keep its depth, surfaced and threw up a cloud of spray. What Bickford muttered was not a blessing, for he was afraid that a keen look-out on the enemy would surely see it in time to evade the attack. But the lop on the seas favoured the *Salmon.*

No sooner were the torpedoes fired than the *Salmon,* whose balance was upset owing to the alterations in weight, dived and dragged the periscope beneath the surface. The captain's anxiety to see the result of his shots can be guessed. His torpedoes were timed to reach the U-boat in about four and a half minutes, and it took him the greater part of this time to adjust the trim of the *Salmon* and bring her to periscope depth again.

If ever a man waited impatiently for the periscope to break clear, it was Bickford. As he gazed into it he saw the conning-tower of the U-boat suddenly disintegrate in a great explosion which carried a mass of debris 200 feet into the air. He was overjoyed. "We've got her!" he called to Wykeham-Martyn, who was the torpedo officer.

At once he surfaced and went full speed to pick up survivors. The area was covered with fuel oil. Slats and bits of wreckage were floating about. Lifebelts were bobbing up and down on the waves.

"Shall we go in for them, sir?" asked members of the crew.

"No," said the captain.

The upper half of a German body floated away supported by a lifebelt.

As a member of the crew stated, it was pretty grim, but no one could tell how many innocent women and children might have been killed by that U-boat if they had missed her.

Steering the *Salmon* clear of the oil, her captain dived. Unwilling to give his position away by making a signal, he refrained from sending news of the destruction of the U-boat until a more opportune moment.

Not until several days had passed did Lieutenant-Commander Bickford wireless his success.

Just before 8 o'clock on the morning of December 12th, the *Salmon* was on the surface when her look-out sighted a Heinkel. As she slid under, Bickford could not understand the German aircraft patrolling for nothing so far from home so early in the morning. It looked as though something was stirring.

Sure enough at 9.30 a.m. the hydrophone operator caught the sounds of a ship. "Engine noises, sir," he reported.

At the moment the *Salmon* was travelling at depth, so her captain steered her higher and signalled for the periscope to be raised. He caught his breath. A great mass was crossing his stern just over a mile away. It was the *Bremen*, on which he had voyaged to the United States and back in 1933, so he knew her well. The only change in her which he could see was that her funnel had been painted a light grey. She was travelling at high speed, and Lieutenant-Commander Bickford at once decided to go up and signal her to stop. If she refused he would open fire on her with his gun. And if she fired on him, he intended to torpedo her.

With the utmost care he examined her through his glasses to see whether she was armed. He could see no signs of a gun. Ten minutes after sighting her he brought the *Salmon* to the surface and the signalman immediately flashed the letter K in the international code for her to stop. There was no reply. Five times in a minute the signal was flashed and ignored.

"Fire a round ahead of her," he ordered the gun-layer, who was busy preparing the gun.

"Aircraft, sir!" called the look-out.

It was a Dornier bearing down on them, just as the shell was pushed into the gun and the breech closed. There was no time to fire the gun. The diving hooter sounded through the boat. The gun's crew flew down, in the words of a petty officer, "as if the devil was after them." The captain slammed the hatch and in thirty seconds the *Salmon* was beneath the surface. Every second the *Bremen* was drawing further away, and by the time the captain had adjusted the trim of the *Salmon* the German liner was beyond range.

"I went deep, as I still considered I was unjustified in firing torpedoes at her," said Lieutenant-Commander Bickford afterwards.

His orders were quite specific. At the beginning of the war the Admiralty had emphasized to all submarine commanding officers that they must adhere rigidly to the international law, and written instructions were given them to this effect. He had read that the *Bremen* had escaped from Murmansk and that she was unarmed, but he had received no special instructions to intercept her. In the circumstances the Admiralty orders stood and he was bound to signal her to stop as a prelude to carrying out the code laid down in the international law.

Yet he was very uneasy in his mind. She was the prize of a lifetime and the pride of Germany. To have her within his grasp and be compelled to let her escape was very disquieting. All he could do was to report to the Admiralty.

His mind was very relieved when he intercepted a message from the Admiralty saying that the *Bremen* was not to be torpedoed.

His action was bound to arouse controversy. The majority of British people gasped with anger that the *Bremen* had been spared. The reports published in praise of the action merely increased the anger. The instincts of the nation were sound. Daily the enemy murdered and raped and plundered and violated all laws ever made by man, and the British people were not so unfamiliar with the Bible as to forget the injunction: "An eye for an eye and a tooth for a tooth." In dealing with gangsters the police take the law into their own hands and over-ride all laws in order that the law—and the people—shall survive. This seems to have been overlooked by those who meticulously observed international laws on land and sea while the enemy ignored them to seize advantages which enabled him to bludgeon humanity. It is probable that if in the early days when the Germans began to scuttle their ships it had been announced that the crews would not be picked up, the scuttling programme would have come to a sudden stop.

One officer who considered the sparing of the *Bremen* was an excellent asset for propaganda misunderstood the temper of the British people. No people are more merciful, but they instinctively realize that only by greater ruthlessness can a ruthless foe be defeated. They are not concerned with the niceties of the law, but they are concerned to see that all their sufferings and losses shall be avenged.

The morning after sighting the *Bremen* the *Salmon* was moving slowly along at periscope depth at 9.45 a.m. when Lieutenant Wykeham-Martyn, who was on duty, caught sight of a ship through the periscope.

"Call the captain," he said to one of the crew.

Within seconds the captain was in the control room.

"There's a little ship over there, sir," said the first lieutenant.

Bickford went to the eyepiece of the periscope. "One, be damned! There's three! Diving stations!" he exclaimed.

The ships were about seven miles away to the north, steaming on a westerly course. The *Salmon* started to close them at full speed and in a quarter of an hour her captain took her up to observe them through the periscope. He was uncertain whether there were two or three heavy ships, whose silhouettes resembled those of the *Admiral Scheer* or the *Graf Spee*. In addition he saw four cruisers—two of the *Hipper* class, one of the *Koenigsberg* class and the other was the *Leipzig*. The main strength of the German Navy was before his eyes. He could hardly credit his luck. Here was a chance which made up for the disappointment of the previous day. That there was anything exceptional in the *Salmon* going in alone to attack the German fleet did not enter his head. His sole concern was whether he could get within striking range.

Driving the *Salmon* at full speed, he strove to close the range. But the German ships were moving at twenty knots and for a time Bickford was in doubt. Then he saw four of them alter course and turn south. His excitement could not be repressed. They were coming straight toward him in line with the *Blücher* leading, followed by the *Leipzig* and *Hipper* cruisers.

Steering west to gain his firing position, Bickford estimated the speed of the ships and watched the range, while Wykeham-Martyn was preparing a salvo of torpedoes and setting them to the depth ordered. Bickford noted that the *Hipper* had swung out of station on to the starboard quarter of the *Leipzig* and as this favoured him, he decided to aim just ahead of the bow of the *Leipzig*. A fighter, whose one desire was to bring about a fleet action, he thought that if he could disable the *Leipzig* and the *Hipper* it might give the Royal Navy a chance to come to grips with the enemy.

"Fire!" he ordered.

The torpedoes hissed through the sea. "Torpedoes running, sir," reported the hydrophone operator.

Altering course at full speed to get away from the firing point before the surface ships could make their counterattack, Bickford took the *Salmon* deep. Four minutes after firing the torpedoes, he heard a loud explosion.

"That's the *Leipzig*," he said happily. A minute later came two more loud explosions.

He drove ahead, listening intently, wondering when the surface ships would begin their attack. Four minutes later he settled on the bottom and stopped everything, motors, fans, cookers, telephones, to prevent any sound reaching the ears listening on the surface for him.

Ships were heard circling furiously over a wide radius. Depth charges were dropped indiscriminately, at too great a distance to do any damage.

Meanwhile the men in the *Salmon* were lying about on the floors and in the bunks. "None of us expected to come out alive," said one of the crew afterwards. "We prayed in our own ways to meet our Maker. I was frightened, but no one but myself knew it. I prayed as I have never prayed before."

Concealing their thoughts from each other, they waited and hoped. Now and again one would whisper to another. All knew that a sound might bring disaster upon them. If it became necessary for one man to move about the ship, he took off his shoes and walked in his stockinged feet to avoid making any noise. Twice the hunters passed over the top of them—and did not know it.

After four hours of this ordeal, the sounds of the hunters died away and the captain carefully brought the *Salmon* up to periscope depth. A quick look showed that the enemy ships had vanished.

Just after dark, at 4.30 p.m. on December 13, 1939— an unlucky day for the enemy, but lucky indeed for Lieutenant-Commander Bickford—the British submarine came to the surface. No enemy ships were to be seen, so that evening the captain celebrated their success by splicing the mainbrace—no men more enjoyed or deserved their tot of rum.

Steering back in the night to the spot where he had attacked the German fleet, Bickford found the surface of the sea over an area of four square miles covered with fuel oil. The smell was overpowering. He had not seen the enemy go down, but there was no doubt she had sunk. Ordering one of the crew to secure a sample by dipping a bucket over the side, Bickford took it back to base as indisputable evidence of his success. The fumes from the oil so choked the interior of the submarine, that the captain was obliged to take her clear of the area in order to blow the gas out.

As she returned home, she received a tremendous welcome along the English coast. Piers were crowded with cheering men. At their base the crew of every ship in the harbour roared their welcome. Mooring beside their mother ship, they climbed on board to find the crew on parade with the captain of the flotilla waiting to greet them. The crew of the *Salmon* fell in while Captain Ruck-Keene addressed them: "You have accomplished a feat that has never been equalled in this war or the last by a British or foreign submarine. I am proud to command a flotilla of which you are a unit and the whole navy is proud of you." He turned to the signalman: "Signalman, hoist the signal, 'Splice the mainbrace!'"

There was a resounding cheer as the men dismissed to drink good luck to the crew of the *Salmon* and their captain.

"The behaviour of both officers and men under the rather trying circumstances of being depth charged was excellent and could not be improved upon," stated Lieutenant-Commander Bickford, who was forthwith promoted to Commander and awarded the D.S.O.

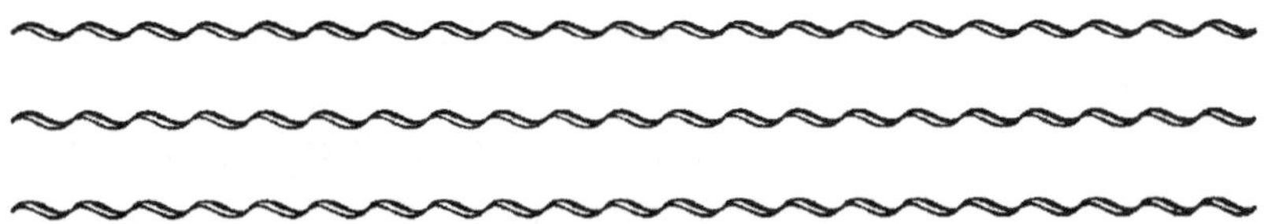

3

THE QUALITY OF MERCY

MEMORIES of April, 1940, when Quisling betrayed Norway and opened the gates of that proud and independent country to the Nazis, tend to grow dim. Great Britain has since suffered much. She has seen the French Government betray its solemn promise not to lay down arms; has watched the British Expeditionary Force fight its way to Dunkirk to escape utter and apparently certain destruction at the hands of the Germans by the most glorious exhibition of sea power the world has ever known; she has risen out of that bitter defeat, phœnix-like, a new nation with a worthy and defiant leader; she has suffered death and destruction in her cities and lovely villages; seen Abyssinia rise again and cast off the Italian bondage; seen Wavell sweep the gigantic Italian armies out of Libya into concentration camps; watched Rommel nearly grasp Egypt before his shattered army fled to Tunisia; has marvelled at the sacrifice and glory of Greece; she has seen the miracle of Russia which has no counterpart since the world began, the traitorous attacks of the Japanese on Pearl Harbour and the Philippines, been misled by the false assurances of military leaders who announced that Hong Kong and Singapore could be held; she has accepted all the sacrifices of the Atlantic battle along with the blessings vouchsafed by her heroic seamen; she has seen the peoples of the United States welded into one people with one purpose in one night—a miracle that justified the heavy cost; she has seen the Chinese enduring and fighting back after five years of torture and destruction matched only by the torture and destruction wrought by the Nazis in Europe and Russia. It is a dark and sombre picture whose magnitude makes it difficult to view in true perspective, and if the light of Nippon gleams in the East, there is a rosy glow in the West to brighten the edge of the gigantic canvas which the gods of war touch with new details night and day. Is it any wonder, then, that the Norwegian scene of 1940 grows dimmer in retrospect? The British people and their allies have since been satiated with horrors and misery, while Europe and Russia have been overwhelmed by cruelties which the United Nations are struggling to sweep away for ever.

But in April, 1940, the vast canvas was almost untouched, with only the lowering skies brushed in above the grisly scene of a crucified Poland and a few lines to indicate the coming of the Nazi terror to

Norway. It was early in April, 1940, that Lieutenant King, D.S.O., D.S.C., took the *Snapper* out to sea and headed for Norway which was then still at peace, unravished by the enemy. The movements of German troops and shipping in the Baltic ports suggested that something was afoot, but until the enemy seized Denmark and sent his convoys to Norway on April 9th no one knew with certainty what new atrocity Hitler would commit.

In the few days before the Germans attacked, Lieutenant King steered the *Snapper* right into those dangerous waters, moving about secretly, keeping a constant watch at the periscope. As he stole into the Skagerrak he observed that the aircraft seemed busier and more numerous, that the big Dornier flying boats flew on their beats at about 500 feet, while the smaller seaplanes prosecuted their search close to the sea. Lieutenant King mentioned such things so impersonally that anyone might be forgiven for failing to realize that the *Snapper* was their target and that her captain was quoting from first-hand experience. He knew what it was to have a squadron of six dive bombers shrieking down out of the sky at him, but he did not worry. His well-trained crew could do a crash dive in half a minute and place a protective belt of water between them and the aircraft bombs which exploded on striking the surface.

With recharged batteries, the *Snapper* floated in the darkness in the early hours of April 12th well in the danger zone, preparatory to starting her usual patrol. Just before 4 o'clock in the morning the lookout detected to the north-east a steamer going north. Dawn was not far away, and Lieutenant King knew that it would bring the recurring aircraft patrols which he was obliged to treat with respect.

"She's close enough to chase," he decided, and called for full speed. He thought it would be simpler and cheaper to sink her with a shell than expend a torpedo. The wake of the *Snapper* grew wider and whiter as she forged ahead. Lieutenant King was in a hurry to overhaul and finish off his quarry. The steamer began to zigzag, not because her master anticipated danger from the submarine, but merely as a precaution. Those seas were regarded as the preserve of Germany, and most German shipmasters considered that the waters were too well mined and patrolled to allow the entry of British or Allied submarines.

The *Snapper* flashed a signal to heave to. The steamer ignored the signal and altered course again. Two or three times the *Snapper* signalled, but the master of the vessel paid no attention. The captain of the *Snapper*, feeling sure that the sound of gunfire would bring the enemy about his ears, was anxious not to fire until he was close enough to destroy her without delay and decamp before the patrols arrived.

After chasing the steamer for seven miles, Lieutenant King put a shot across her bows. At once the steamer began to lose way and the captain of the *Snapper* saw her break the Nazi merchant flag. It transpired later that the German captain was convinced by the markings on the conning-tower that the *Snapper* was a Swedish submarine and it was a bit of a shock when she drew close and a voice shouted to him to abandon ship. "As you wish," came the reply from the German ship.

The captain of the *Snapper* watched the German ship intently for any treacherous move. The crew manned the gun which was trained on the enemy, the Lewis gunner stood on the bridge with alert eyes. The Germans did nothing, they made no attempt to launch a boat, they simply stopped under the guns of the *Snapper*.

"Put a burst over the masts," ordered the captain to the Lewis gunner, who promptly obeyed.

Still the Germans made no attempt to abandon ship.

"Fire one round at the forepeak," ordered the captain, to the gunlayer below.

"Aye, aye, sir," replied the gunlayer, who carried out the order.

If the Germans had been loath to move before, they moved swiftly now, for a big burst of flame followed the explosion of the shell. They dived desperately over the side. As it happened they carried a cargo of aviation spirit and knew that the shell meant death to them unless they left the ship instantly. Swift as they were, they were not all swift enough to beat the gush of fire.

Against the recurring atrocities of German submarine commanders the action of Lieutenant King at that moment shone out as brightly as a beacon on a dark night. Here were enemies who had refused to obey orders and launch their boat and abandon ship. They had refused to heave to when he had signalled them. In similar circumstances the Germans would have had no compunction in leaving their enemies to their fate, if they did not actually hasten their death by turning machine guns on them while they were in the water.

Lieutenant King, however, true to the great tradition of the Royal Navy, manœuvred the *Snapper* until he succeeded in picking up every man he could find, six in all out of a crew of seven. The seventh man was never seen. He must have been snuffed out like a moth in a flame.

Four of the Germans were unharmed, but two of them were suffering badly from the shock of burns and exposure. Sending the unharmed Germans down through the conning-tower hatchway, the captain ordered the injured men to be taken carefully below. It was no easy matter handling them down the narrow hatchway, but one was gently lowered and put into a bunk. They were manipulating the other through the hatchway when an aircraft flew toward them at the same time as a patrolling trawler was sighted coming to see what the gunfire meant.

Lieutenant King was right in thinking that he would not remain unmolested long after firing his gun. He just had time to get the last injured German on board and take the *Snapper* under, when the aircraft arrived.

Slowly the *Snapper* started to steal away from the danger point. The sea was like glass, with conditions as ideal for hunting submarines as the enemy could desire. Now and again the captain of the *Snapper* took a quick look through the periscope. He saw the trawler hanging round the burning steamer, which quickly burned out and sank. He caught brief glimpses of dive bombers patrolling the area to look for him. But the trawler fortunately failed to contact him and it was about five hours after firing at the *Moonsund* before an aircraft attack developed. The bombs, however, did no damage.

While this attack was going on, the German prisoners showed no sign of fear. They seemed surprised that they had been picked up at all and were full of gratitude for the kind treatment they received on board. Their wet clothes were stripped off and they were provided with garments collected from the crew until such time as their own clothes were dried for them. A generous dose of Navy rum and cups of hot tea soon restored their circulation.

The two injured men, however, were far gone, and as the *Snapper* moved slowly under the surface while the enemy above and in the air sought to destroy her and her crew, the British sailors, who did not know from one minute to another when death might rain down on them and overtake them, fought desperately to try to save the lives of the two Germans. They ransacked the medicine chest and did all they could to rally them, but the men failed to respond to the treatment and eventually died.

All day the *Snapper* moved beneath the glassy seas in that danger zone. That evening the captain, assembling the crew along with the four German prisoners, solemnly read the burial service over the dead bodies of the enemy. It was a moving scene, the young British officer praying for the souls of his enemies before consigning them to the deep. It was a scene to live in British history and make future generations proud of the traditions of their race and the Royal Navy. In the very heat of battle, while the Germans were committing atrocities which stamped them as less than the brutes of the jungle, a young British naval officer was merciful enough to rescue his enemies and noble enough to read the burial service over them before their bodies were buried in the sea.

Closing the prayer book, Lieutenant King steered the *Snapper* to the surface. The conning-tower hatch was opened and the dead reverently passed up into the clean night air. Then with bared heads the captain and officers and some members of the crew stood by while the dead started on their last voyage and the sea closed over them for ever.

An unsuccessful attack on a steamer just before 2 o'clock one morning, brought the *Snapper* to the edge of destruction. She was proceeding on the surface away from the scene, when two destroyers suddenly appeared out of the darkness. Steaming at twenty knots, they were exactly 200 yards away when the *Snapper* crash dived to safety. It was much too near.

Twelve hours later Lieutenant King hit a merchant ship with one torpedo and spent a lively time dodging the depth charges which followed. Next day he stole upon a convoy making for the Norwegian coast and heard some of his torpedoes strike home. The explosions led him to believe that he hit two ships, but he was hunted so fiercely for the rest of the day that he could not see what happened.

The very nature of a submarine's work makes it difficult to verify results, for the firing of a torpedo usually calls forth a fierce counterattack which keeps the submarine under for long periods and demands all the skill and courage and endurance of the captain and crew to evade. Considerable time may therefore elapse before it is possible to learn the fate and identity of any ships attacked.

Certainly Lieutenant W. D. King struck hard against the Nazis during that patrol, which won for him the D.S.O. as well as the high praise of Sir Max Horton who said: "The rescue of the survivors of S.S. *Moonsund* was in accordance with the best traditions of the submarine service."

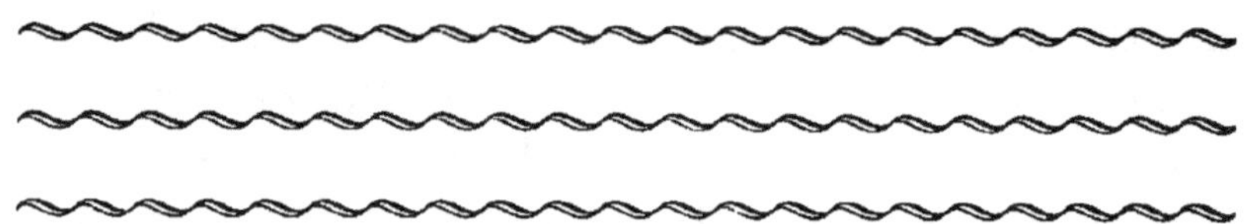

4

A LUCKY LOOPHOLE

THE fact that Lieutenant-Commander G. D. A. Gregory, D.S.O. and Bar, who was born in Glasgow on October 8, 1909, came of a line whose forebears went to sea in their youth probably influenced his parents into selecting his naval career. Being anxious to settle him in life, they sent him at the age of fourteen to the Royal Naval College at Dartmouth to fit him for the Navy.

When war broke out he was the captain of the *Sturgeon.* Unlike those more fortunate submariners who were able to spend their first Christmas of the war at their bases, he was patrolling in Heligoland Bight during Christmas week, and while the usual Christmas festivities were denied him and his crew, he was nevertheless determined that he would at least hold a special service on Christmas morning. Lacking hymn books on board, he started a competition among the crew to see who could write out the Christmas carols and hymns from memory. The memories of the men were none too good, but they did their best. Some remembered a line or two of this carol, others a few lines of that, while some recollected whole verses. Between them the crew of forty managed to recall the words of three carols for inclusion in the morning service. Several members of the crew could play mouth organs, so the captain selected the two best players to accompany the crew in the carols, and from time to time on Christmas Eve soft snatches of carols might have been heard in the *Sturgeon* as the two players practised pianissimo to ensure that they made no mistake.

On Christmas morning about 10 o'clock the captain took the *Sturgeon* to the bottom of the Heligoland Bight and stopped her. Then he called all the officers and crew into the fore ends for the service. Seldom has a Christmas service been held in a stranger place. They were locked in their steel tube on the bottom of the sea in the very heart of enemy waters. Death and destruction lurked round them. No one could tell when the enemy might strike. But for the moment all thoughts of the enemy were banished from their minds. Neither Hitler nor his cohorts could prevent this little band of Britons from observing Christmas Day as their fathers and forefathers had done before them.

They were indeed a weird congregation. Many had scrubby beards which gave them a very unkempt appearance. Their garb, too, was anything but the neat suit usually worn on Christmas Day. They were dressed in the queerest clothes ever collected out of a junk bag, some had on football jerseys, others wore brown overalls, some were in dirty grey flannels and what were once white naval jerseys; there were men in sea-boots, some in white canvas shoes, others in ordinary shoes, while the captain himself was dressed in several sweaters, cord trousers and snow boots.

He stood there, nearly six feet tall, a serious look in his blue eyes, as he opened his prayer book and turned the pages to the Collect for Christmas Day. The light of the fore ends lit the contours of his nose, mouth and chin; it glinted on his dark hair in which a few gray hairs already peeped above the ears. He looked at the crew who stood reverently around him and in a calm, even voice read the Collect and the prayers for the day. Then he led the entire crew in the Lord's Prayer and announced the first carol. So the voices of the whole crew rang out in praise and mingled with the strains of the mouth organs, to reverberate through the boat that was many fathoms deep in the Heligoland Bight. There was nothing incongruous about it. They were modern crusaders fighting barbarism in order to preserve Christian civilisation and paying a solemn tribute to their Faith. The sound of their voices singing carols pulsed through the enemy waters. But if the Germans heard, they must have thought they were dreaming, for the religious service held by the captain of the *Sturgeon* at the bottom of the sea continued to the last Amen without interruption.

"It was most impressive," was the captain's description of it.

Known among his intimates in the service as David, he torpedoed a ship in November, 1939, and for months afterwards the gods of chance eyed him askance. It was depressing to go out on patrol after patrol without sinking a ship. There were periodical excitements caused by enemy aircraft or anti-submarine ships, but the longed-for view of a great ship coming into his sights was denied him.

In August, 1940, he slipped from his depot ship and steamed away in the direction of Norway. Very carefully he studied his orders. They were quite definite. He was to patrol on a certain line, but they did not state where the line was to end. Now, a line, as everyone knows, may be extended to infinity. The captain of the *Sturgeon* was aware that the eastern end of the line led into shallows which would bring him off the Skaw on the northerly tip of Denmark, where there was likely to be good hunting. There were no instructions that his patrol line was to end where the shallows began.

That was a mistake, but it gave him a glorious loophole through which he decided to dive with the utmost celerity, and allow neither shoals nor the possibility of mines to stop him. Quite unwittingly, he was offered the great chance of making the Germans pay for a trifling slip, and he seized upon it with delight. There was no lack of the offensive spirit so far as he was concerned.

He thought of all the fruitless patrols of the past months. The crew certainly needed a fillip. It was about time he had another success to keep them in good heart. So with these motives in his mind, he adopted the Nelson touch, and followed the line to its logical conclusion. Even the elements conspired to help him. A big gale sprang up and increased the drift of the current, which enabled him to reach a point off the Skaw much quicker than normally.

By the time he arrived in the Skaw the gale blew itself out and left a heavy swell which made conditions difficult for attack. Throughout the morning and afternoon of September 2nd, he waited and hoped that something might come his way. Nothing did, except anti-submarine trawlers and aircraft, and they were the last things he wished to see. Towards evening he was becoming a little despondent. Whether his conscience was quite clear about following the line, only he can tell. Some little element of doubt in his mind may have added to his despondency.

Twilight came. The sun set, and it grew darker. About 7 o'clock a seaplane flew over and would not go away. It kept flying around the position occupied by the *Sturgeon*, but whether the pilot detected the submarine or not was a moot point. Half an hour passed.

"Engine noises, bearing red 130, sir," reported the hydrophone operator, who heard a ship.

The captain swung the periscope in that direction, but there was nothing to be seen. The sun was well below the horizon. The whole horizon was now quite dark, except a lighter patch to the north-west.

Patiently the captain waited, wondering what was coming along. In a few minutes the silhouette of a torpedo-boat came into his field of vision against the light horizon.

"Diving stations!" he ordered.

Another minute or two passed, then a large transport was seen about three miles distant. It was passing away from the *Sturgeon*, and could only be reached by a long shot.

The men stood to their stations. The torpedo tubes were blown up by turning on the compressed air to force water into them from the interior tanks.

Another torpedo-boat appeared, followed by three or four small merchantmen.

Already the captain of the *Sturgeon* had speeded up and was turning on his firing course. The captain studied the transport. "I saw that she was very large and fast, and I had to guess her course and speed and range. I could see nothing except her black shape. It was pure guesswork, based on my knowledge of the speed of that sort of ship," he once said, in describing the attack.

He stood there in the control-room, full of excitement, but no one would have imagined it from his mask of a face, for he had been trained to appear calm in all circumstances, as is the way of the Navy. He intended to fire torpedoes at the transport and, if his luck held, have a shot at the other ships.

The periscope was lowered until he judged the transport was approaching the bearing on which he wanted to fire.

"Up periscope!" he ordered, and waited for the target to creep across his field of vision. He saw the silhouette slide up to the central line engraved upon the glass.

"Fire!" he said, and the torpedoes sped on their way. That, to him, was the most peculiar sensation of all. He knew the torpedoes were rushing toward the ship, but he no longer had any control over them. All he could do was to wait and wait and wait.

He altered course toward the other ships just as they turned away and prevented him from attacking them. An aircraft flew over, and he wondered if the pilot had seen the tracks of the torpedoes.

About five minutes after he fired there was a slight bang, which was heard throughout the boat. The *Sturgeon* jolted at the shock. The men in the control-room glanced at each other and grins spread over their faces.

"Up periscope!" ordered the captain, stooping down with his eye at the eyepiece, and straightening up as the periscope broke through the surface. He saw an enormous column of black smoke rising up and up for 2,000 feet above the ship, with gigantic sparks shooting through it.

"We've got a hit," said the captain. "She's a big ship." He turned to his first lieutenant. "Have a look," he added.

The first lieutenant looked and was satisfied, so the captain beckoned the coxswain. "Come on," he said, and the coxswain gazed at the doomed ship.

Resuming his place at the periscope, the captain saw the transport burst into flames from stem to stern. The flames grew brighter and more intense. Yellow-white tongues licked high into the air. An occasional fireball shot up. Every now and then one of the torpedo-boats passed between the *Sturgeon* and the burning ship. The flames were reflected upon the heaving seas. It was now pitch dark. He watched the torpedo-boats starting and stopping to pick up survivors.

Directly the captain of the *Sturgeon* saw the ship settling he dived deep to reload the torpedo-tubes, and came up again about four miles away, breaking surface right in the beam of a searchlight from one of the torpedo-boats. It was an anxious moment. Fortunately, the torpedo-boat was so busy rescuing survivors that it failed to notice the *Sturgeon*.

The transport had gone, and the torpedo-boats were busy lighting the spot with the searchlights.

Stockholm reported later that the ships were picking up survivors till daylight, and that great numbers of drowned German soldiers were washed up on the Swedish coast.

Thus Lieutenant-Commander Gregory followed his line to success. There is no doubt that the intention in drafting his orders was to limit his patrol to the beginning of the declared area, and there was a whisper that he had to toe the line and got a bit of a wigging about it when he returned. But what could the Admiralty do? The orders were specific, and he had carried them out to the letter. He had struck a mighty blow that had shaken up the enemy throughout the Kattegat, and his prowess and skill were acclaimed. As for the loophole in his orders, he slipped through it to such good purpose that he fully deserved the Bar to his earlier D.S.O. which was awarded to him.

The amusing thing is that he denied a knowledge of Euclid, yet he was canny enough to realise that a straight line may be continued to infinity!

Once, after an attack of influenza, he had to call on Admiral Max Horton, or Admiral "S," as he was known in the service of which he was then the head. The Admiral's tanned face puckered in a smile as he eyed him. "You're not looking very well," he said.

"I've had 'flu, sir," was the reply.

"Take three weeks' leave. I'll send someone up to relieve you," said the Admiral.

Which goes to explain why all the officers and men in the submarine service worshipped him. He knew all the answers to all the questions. Good work won his warmest praise, but he could be very sharp and critical if necessary.

There was a day when Lieutenant-Commander Gregory saw the coxswain entering the boat with a lot of green tomatoes. "Why are you carrying those green tomatoes?" asked the captain.

"Would you like one when they are ripe, sir?" replied the cockswain.

"I would," said the captain.

Ten days later the coxswain appeared in the wardroom and laid upon the table ten lovely tomatoes that were perfectly ripe. They had been nestling cosily in his hat all the time!

Another time the *Sturgeon* acquired a new cook, whose culinary accomplishments were quite unknown. One of the first things he had to do was to boil eggs for the whole crew.

"How long do I boil them?" he inqured.

"Three minutes," replied a rating.

In due course the eggs were served—absolutely solid.

"I can't understand it," said the cook. "I did what you said, and gave 'em three minutes!"

It transpired that he had multiplied forty eggs by three minutes and had boiled them for two hours.

The time came when the captain of the *Sturgeon*, who had been on unbroken patrol longer than any other officer, was due for a spell ashore. He prepared to take the *Sturgeon* out for his last patrol before handing her over to someone else. "May I have *carte blanche* to go where I like in the Skagerrak, sir?" he asked the captain of his flotilla.

Captain "S" quizzed him. "All right," he agreed.

So Lieutenant-Commander Gregory took the

Sturgeon back to the scene of her greatest triumph. The first night he surfaced to recharge in the middle of a Danish fishing fleet. Some of the vessels were lighted, others were not, and the situation was a little eerie.

Suddenly the look-out reported a white wave coming up from astern—the bow-wave of a ship at night is nearly always seen before the ship herself is detected. Gazing aft through his binoculars, he saw what he thought was a big destroyer. Breaking the charge and slipping in the port tail clutch, he ordered the torpedoes to be prepared, and waited to attack the oncoming ship. The *Sturgeon* was in a bad position, silhouetted against a light horizon; the enemy moved against a black background, and was difficult to make out. As the distance lessened, he realized that it was not a destroyer at all, but two anti-submarine trawlers bearing down on him, no more than 800 yards away, much too close for his peace of mind.

"Dive!" he called, and as the officer of the watch and the look-out dropped through the conning-tower hatch, he followed and pulled the cover down after pressing the diving hooter. In seconds the ballast tanks were flooding, and the *Sturgeon* was pushing her bow down in a crash dive, which he levelled out at 60 feet.

Stopping all the machinery, he waited for the depth-charges. He guessed they would be too accurate for his liking. Undoubtedly the *Sturgeon* had been seen, and the Germans were bent on destroying her.

No haphazard attack followed, but a cold-blooded, merciless stalk, which was the worst attack the captain of the *Sturgeon* had ever endured. The enemies were not wasting their depth-charges plastering the ocean; they were saving them to get one right home.

A third trawler joined the hunt. In vain the captain of the *Sturgeon* turned the stern of his boat and tried to steal away. The enemy held him fast and would not let him go. For some time the hunt went on, with the captain of the *Sturgeon* doing his best to baffle the enemy and trying all the tricks he knew.

The crisis called forth all the skill and knowledge of Lieutenant-Commander G. D. A. Gregory, D.S.O. and Bar, and eventually enabled him to outwit the Germans and bring his last patrol of the *Sturgeon* to a happy ending.

5

TORPEDOING

THE *KARLSRUHE*

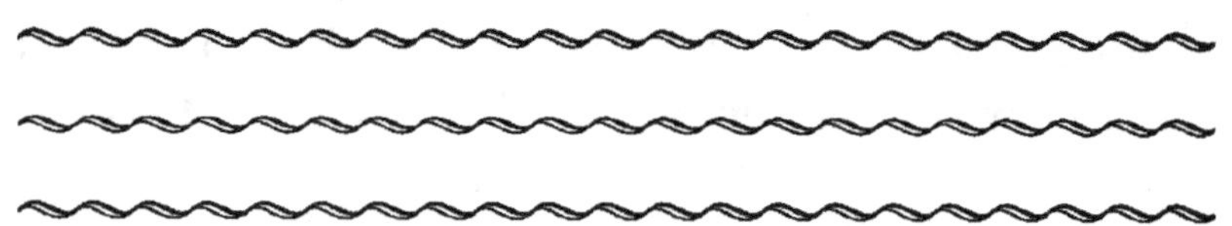

To BE bound hand and foot, at the mercy of the most ruthless enemy the world has known, would be an ordeal that few men could face with equanimity; yet the position from which Lieutenant-Commander Christopher Haynes Hutchinson, D.S.O., extricated himself was very similar. Not that he or the members of his crew were actually roped, but the *Truant*, in which they did such good work, was tied up as effectively as a man who is chained by the legs.

Starting out on that patrol, they lurked about outside territorial waters in the hope of intercepting the *Altmark*. Lieutenant-Commander Hutchinson would have given anything to avenge the inhuman treatment of the *Altmark's* prisoners, who by this time had been rescued by the *Cossack*, but the German prison ship did not come within his ken, and a signal sent him hunting elsewhere.

At first sight the new position seemed to bristle with danger, for there were what appeared to be myriads of floating mines. They were, in fact, large fishermen's floats some four feet in diameter, which the uninitiated would consider to be as harmless as toy balloons.

Fishermen's floats, nevertheless, may prove to be a deadly menace to a submarine. They cannot explode like a mine, it is true, but they have ropes attached to the nets they buoy, and ropes in the sea are a nightmare to a submarine captain, for if they happen to entangle the propellers they can truss up his ship securely and leave her lying helpless.

Just half an hour after midnight the *Truant* was moving along the surface in a fog, when she ran into this area that was thick with fishermen's buoys. They were everywhere, and before she could get clear, numerous ropes were wound round her port propeller. The thing that all submarine captains dread, fouled propellers, had happened in the worst possible position, right in enemy waters, where the foe would be down on the *Truant* with guns and depth-charges and bombs as soon as daylight came. Unless her captain could win free before dawn, the position looked ominous.

He started the fight to disentangle the *Truant* from those terrible ropes, driving her port engine hard ahead and astern to try to unwind or cut them. For hour after hour the struggle went on. She dragged behind her the floats which tied her up. Now and again one drifted away to hearten the captain and let him know there was one bond the less to sever. The chronometer indicated 3 o'clock, then 4 o'clock, with the propeller still fouled. Using all his dexterity, he manœuvred the *Truant* to unravel the tangle round her shaft. By 6 o'clock only one float remained, but all his efforts failed to shift it.

Never before had he been grateful for fog, but he was grateful that morning, for it cloaked his movements and offered him a sporting chance of escaping the notice of the enemy when it grew light. By 7 o'clock it was not possible to see for more than three hundred yards, and he determined to cut away the last float by hand. Filling the forward tanks and blowing out the tanks aft, he adjusted the trim of the *Truant* until her bow was under water and her propellers were above the surface. Then Lieutenant R. D. Whiteway-Wilkinson, with a line round his body to prevent him from being washed away by the rough sea, went down the casing into the water, accompanied by a rating to aid him, and with the waves breaking over him most of the time, hacked at the rope with a knife until he freed the propeller. It was one of those unknown acts of gallantry that are considered to be all in the day's work.

A much nastier experience befell the *Truant* on another patrol. She was running on the surface at twelve knots, just after 3 o'clock in the morning, with Lieutenant Whiteway-Wilkinson on the bridge, when the whole ship shook under the shock of an explosion. Nothing resembling a ship or a mine was in sight, but when the explosion occurred the first lieutenant saw a dull flash to starboard near the bow. The strange thing was that the surface of the sea remained quite undisturbed; there was no upheaval of water, nor even a splash.

What caused the explosion is a mystery, but there is no doubt that the *Truant* came near to destruction. The force of the explosion sheared through some metal pins, and flung two of the *Truant's* torpedoes out of their tubes. Only the efficiency of the safety devices prevented those torpedoes from blowing the *Truant* to pieces, so she really had a treble escape.

No wonder Lieutenant-Commander Hutchinson was told it was better to be born lucky than rich, especially in war.

He was patrolling close off the Danish coast about 10 o'clock one night when he signalled a darkened steamer to stop and told her not to use her radio. Instead of stopping she increased speed and sent out an S O S, whereupon the *Truant* fired two rounds of high-explosive shells, which hit the bridge. "I stop," she signalled, and sent out a wireless call that she was held up by an English submarine. The *Truant* promptly put three more shells into her to silence the radio, and in three minutes she listed and began to settle, while the crew took to the boats and started to pull hard for the shore.

The steamer was the *Hugo Stinnes*, whose master was taken prisoner. "Give me a new pair of trousers," he demanded of Lieutenant-Commander Hutchinson as soon as he got on board the *Truant*.

"Why?" inquired the puzzled captain of the *Truant*.

"You would want a new pair, too, if you'd had a shell through your cabin to wake you up," said the discomfited German master.

Without doubt the most thrilling experience of Lieutenant-Commander Hutchinson occurred on April 9, 1940, when he shook the German naval command by sinking the *Karlsruhe*. That was the day on which the Nazis started to invade Norway. It was just after 5 o'clock in the afternoon when he sighted three torpedo-boats and prepared to attack them. Within a few minutes, however, they nullified his efforts by altering course and steaming away at 22 knots.

An hour later, at 6.33 p.m., the hull of a cruiser pushed over the horizon, and at once Lieutenant-Commander Hutchinson turned the *Truant* to attack her. She proved to be a cruiser of the *Koln* class, protected by an escort of at least three destroyers. Nineteen minutes after she was first sighted she turned away, and presented a much more difficult target to the *Truant*, which was then 4,500 yards distant.

Lieutenant-Commander Hutchinson's observations gave her a speed of 23 knots. In making an attack he usually relied upon his own eye and judgment, and used his instruments as an emergency check. He was so determined to sink the cruiser, which now presented a most difficult target, that he decided to fire a salvo of torpedoes at her. At 6.56 p.m. he fired, and a minute later, when the last torpedo hissed into the sea, the first one was two-thirds of a mile away speeding toward the target.

Firing this salvo naturally upset the trim of the *Truant*. As she went down the first explosion reached the ears of the captain, about three minutes after firing the first torpedo. This loud explosion was followed by another, which was succeeded a few seconds later by a third. With the explosions came the sound of rending metal, to indicate beyond doubt that the attack had been successful.

Raising his periscope for a quick sight, the captain saw two destroyers rushing down on him, and dived to avoid their attack. The first pattern of depth-charges nearly caught the *Truant*. They were so close that the explosions made the forehatch jump open, letting in a surge of water before it slammed back into place again. Had the clips which secured it been faulty, they would have snapped under the strain, and the *Truant* would have joined the *Karlsruhe* on the bottom.

Down the *Truant* dived to avoid the depth-charges until she was at the limit of her range. The destroyers, skilful hunters, were hard on her track. The captain could hear the depth-charges exploding, after which the destroyers stopped to listen for the movements of the *Truant*.

The cook was coolness personified. He sat in the control-room calmly peeling potatoes, and as the depth-charges dropped he would toss a potato into the air to let it fall into the bucket with a splash to coincide with the explosion. His action so heartened the crew that the captain mentioned him in despatches.

The captain, doing his best to counter the attacks, went steadily ahead at half-speed. He was afraid to change speed for fear that the alteration in the sound give away his position. Lights were switched off and all other machinery stopped. Time and again the captain changed course, but the Germans heard him and could not be shaken off.

"The enemy appeared to be uncomfortably efficient at hunting, and most persistent. I hoped forlornly that they would retire after dark on more important business," he remarked afterwards.

All the time water leaked into the boat and drained aft. Under normal conditions it could easily have been pumped out, but the captain dared not start the pump, because the noise and oily water would have betrayed him. In consequence the *Truant* moved with her stern well down, owing to the added weight of water. The hydroplanes had received a jolt which put them temporarily out of action, and the general shock made the magnetic compasses behave in the most fantastic manner. Having been obliged to stop the gyro-compass to avoid noise, the captain had no idea where he was going.

About 9.30 that night things quietened down, and the captain began to hope that the hunters had drawn off. Going ahead for another fifteen minutes and hearing nothing, he concluded it was safe to go to periscope depth to have a look round. The hunters, however, were merely lying low. Before he could get up to periscope depth their charges drove him deep again.

For another two hours the *Truant* proceeded at depth. Her batteries were depleted. She had been down for nineteen hours, and the air was so foul that the crew were finding it difficult to breathe. As the sounds of the enemy could no longer be heard, the captain decided to take her to the surface, where he discovered that his pursuers had given up the chase.

He stopped the *Truant* and turned over both main engines to recharging the batteries in the shortest time. Then he was confronted with the problem of getting away. He had no compasses to guide him; the night was dark, but daylight in two hours' time would necessitate diving again; no star was out by which he could steer. Remembering that the wind blew from the north-east on the previous day, he decided to clear this dangerous area by going down-wind until the stars came out. His judgment was justified, and directly the stars appeared he was able to set his course.

It is worth recording, to the glory of the Royal Navy in general and the submarine service in particular, that after such a gruelling time Lieutenant-Commander Hutchinson advised the Admiralty of the multiple damage the *Truant* had suffered and, as he had some torpedoes left, calmly inquired whether he could remain at sea. He was ordered to return.

The crew were rather exhausted, but they soon set to work repairing the damage. By the time the *Truant* reached base many of her minor defects had been made good. Lieutenant-Commander Hutchinson looked at her with an appraising eye. Along the middle seam of the pressure hull was a slight red mark that only the expert would notice: it was a rust mark, which showed how the pressure hull had been forced to give slightly under the great weight of the sea in the depths where she had found sanctuary; but the work of the shipbuilders stood that supreme test.

This is the authentic account of how Commander Hutchinson, to give him his present rank, sank the *Karlsruhe* and won the D.S.O.

6

ESCAPE OF THE *TRIUMPH*

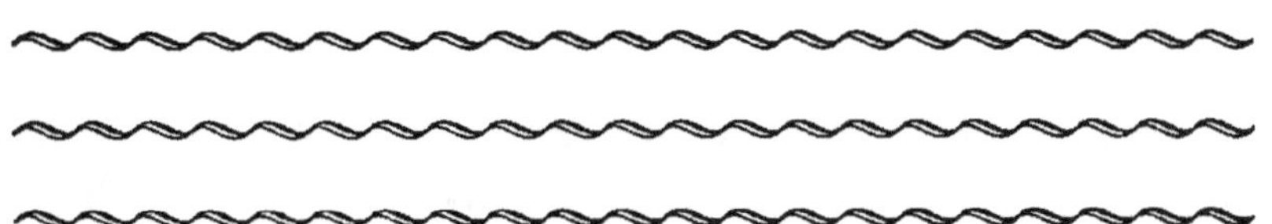

SHIPS of all nations, strewn over the sea-bed, testify to the destructive effect of German mines, and the enemy's developments of the magnetic mine and the acoustic mine were fraught with unexpected perils. Yet it was in October, 1916, that Mr. C. Marshall of the United States applied for a patent for a magnetic mine; and during the last war Sir Frank Smith, aided by other British scientists, designed for the Admiralty a magnetic mine which proved effective. Believing that this type of mine would destroy British sea power, the Germans toiled on it for years in secret.

With sublime courage, Lieutenant-Commander J. G. D. Ouvry and Lieutenant-Commander R. C. Lewis, assisted by Lieutenant J. E. M. Glenny, Chief Petty Officer C. E. Baldwin and Able Seaman A. Verncombe, worked by torch-light in the mud of the Thames in November, 1939, to take one of these mines to pieces in order to discover its secrets, and the senior officers were awarded the D.S.O., Lieutenant Glenny received the D.S.C., while their assistants won the D.S.M. "For great courage and skill in securing and stripping live enemy mines, without regard for their own safety," to quote the *London Gazette* of December 23, 1939.

The German failure to discover a defence against the mine led Hitler to boast of this secret weapon which could not be countered; yet in a few weeks British scientists discovered how to protect ships against this new menace.

The mine is worked by a magnetic needle, which is attracted by any steel ship that comes within a certain radius. As the needle moves, it operates a contact which explodes the mine. The problem which the British scientists faced was to demagnetize a ship so that it ceased to attract and move the magnetic needle in the mine. They found it could be done quite simply by running a specially-charged steel rope round the hull of a vessel. Known as the degaussing gear, this is now fitted to all British ships, and it enables them to sail in safety over a magnetic minefield. The defence against the acoustic mine, which is actuated by the sound made by the propellers of ships, was likewise found in a short time by British scientists.

Despite these defences, mines remain a deadly peril, and it would seem to be impossible for a submarine to run one down and escape destruction. Nevertheless, this is exactly what the *Triumph* did some three months after the outbreak of war. At that time she was commanded by Lieutenant Commander J. W. McCoy, a skilful submarine captain who brought a logical brain to bear upon his hazardous profession. Blessed with the ability to regard things objectively, he was undisturbed by the risks he ran in those earlier patrols. His mental poise was proved early in the war when, twice hunted by torpedo-boats and trawlers and forced to dive to a crushing depth in order to escape, he wrote of the hunters: "It is not known why depth-charges were not dropped, as on two occasions they appeared to be very close and only lacked the courage of their convictions."

That was written after he had spent a dozen hours in the depths repairing his steering-gear.

In the latter days of December, 1939, the crew of the *Triumph* busied themselves in preparation for their next patrol, examining all the gear, making adjustments, taking in stores. While millions of people crowded the shops buying presents and looking forward to spending a happy Christmas by their own firesides, the crew of the *Triumph* stowed away their provisions for the forthcoming days, and on December 23, 1939, left their base to grapple with the enemy.

At 11 o'clock on Boxing night they surfaced and started to recharge on the starboard engine, while they went ahead on the other. There were occasional flurries of snow, and a full moon appeared fitfully through the scudding clouds.

Lieutenant L. W. A. Bennington, the officer of the watch, was on the bridge when, at 11.6 p.m., he saw but twenty feet ahead of the *Triumph's* bow a huge mine about six feet in diameter that glinted like copper in the moonlight. It floated up into sight on the crest of a swell. Instantaneously he put the helm hard-a-starboard to escape it.

The *Triumph* had no chance to avoid the mine, no time even to start to swing under the influence of her rudder in that short distance. Less than three seconds after Lieutenant Bennington caught sight of the mine, the *Triumph* struck it with her bow.

There was a great explosion. A blast of air hit the officer and look-out as a sheet of flame leapt fifty feet into the sky.

Lieutenant Bennington expected the *Triumph* to sink at once. It seemed incredible that she should remain afloat, yet she did. Another queer thing was that although there was a mighty gush of flame when the mine exploded, he did not see the usual column of water shoot up into the sky. It says much for his coolness in that crisis—within seconds, as it seemed, of being blown to pieces—that he made a mental note of these peculiarities. The blast, too, was not terrific. "It was just medium," he said afterwards. Some happy combination of circumstances saved him and the look-out from injury.

The men below felt the *Triumph* lurch and shudder. The noise inside the ship was not very loud. In fact, one of the men who was sleeping in his hammock in the torpedo compartment slept through the explosion, and wondered why he was roused to go to his diving station. The others thought they had been hit by a shell, and had no idea it was a mine.

The captain of the *Triumph* moved quickly forward through the ship to see what was wrong. Everything seemed to be as usual until he came to the bulkhead leading to the torpedo space. Here the water-tight door was jammed and could not be unfastened. Opening the door in the escape chamber, he passed through into the torpedo compartment, where he found half-a-dozen lights had gone out and some of the floor plates had shifted. The water-tight doors leading to the fore ends were shut as usual, and beyond that the captain did not seek to explore, but hastened to the bridge to find out what had occurred.

"We struck a mine!" said the officer of the watch, who pointed to the bows. The captain gazed ahead and saw the plates of the pressure hull all crumpled and the wireless aerial down.

"Signal to base," he instructed the wireless operator.

His coolness and the coolness of every man on board the *Triumph* in that crisis was an expression of their high courage. Commenting on it afterwards, Lieutenant-Commander McCoy said: "The conduct of officers and men was that nothing very extraordinary had happened, and they carried out their duties in a normal manner."

The *Triumph's* call for help sent five destroyers speeding through the night to her rescue, news which the captain of the submarine was thankful to receive.

Away at base the duty officer looked at the map on the wall in the operations-room, giving the latest position of the submarines. Quietly his incisive voice dictated the necessary messages.

It was impossible for the destroyers to come up with the *Triumph* before midday on December 27th. Meanwhile it was necessary for the captain to find out how badly the *Triumph* was damaged, and to do what he could to keep her afloat until she could make port.

Nothing could have been more misleading than the small signs of damage showing inside the submarine. At that moment she was a ship without a bow, for some eighteen feet had been completely blown off by the explosion, and if the water-tight doors had not been closed or the bulkheads had been less strongly built, she would have plunged straight to the bottom for ever. The full magnitude of the damage could not be seen from the bridge in the moonlight. The seas and the shadows tended to obscure it, and it could only be conjectured.

At once Lieutenant-Commander McCoy sought to discover exactly how bad it was. His keen brain told him that the Triumph could not run down a mine without suffering serious consequences. The main facts were that she was still afloat, and was apparently undamaged as far forward as the bulkhead and doors on the far side of the torpedo flats. The question was —what lay behind those closed doors leading to the fore ends? Would an uncontrollable rush of water come through to overwhelm the men who volunteered to open them and perhaps carry the *Triumph* to the seabed? Risk lurked behind those closed doors. Whether it was deadly, or whether it could be dealt with, no man on board could tell. The first essential to safety was to find out. A quick calculation told the captain of the *Triumph* that he had enough buoyancy in hand to support a considerable weight of extra water. Unknown risks were, of course, inseparable from war. Exercising the greatest care, the butterfly nut holding the clip on the port door, which happened to be the only clip fastened, was unscrewed. If there had been an overwhelming force of water behind the door, it would have started to force its way through as the clip was eased. As nothing like this happened, the captain knew that it was safe to open the door.

But what they found was bad enough. The water was flooding eighteen inches above the floor plates, it was gushing through several leaks. Without delay they started to locate the leaks and plug them to the best of their ability. The bulkhead at the fore end was their first line of defence beyond which the captain now knew that all the damage lay. So long as this bulkhead held, the *Triumph* had a reasonable chance of getting back. Utilizing what material was available, the British seamen propped and strengthened it as much as they could.

Meanwhile they got a pump to work to cope with the water coming into the fore ends. Running the pump alternatively on the starboard side and then on the port side, they managed to keep the water down. For a time, when the inflow exceeded the capacity of the pump, things began to look dangerous, but the pump managed to get on top of its job again.

Foreseeing this danger, Lieutenant-Commander McCoy prepared to meet it scientifically in the only way that lay within his power—by turning on the compressed air until the pressure of the air inside the compartment was great enough to hold the water back. Meanwhile he had an air-pressure gauge rigged inside the compartment so that a glance would disclose any dangerous alteration in pressure. He was determined not to use compressed air unless absolutely obliged, for he did not know how far the structure of the submarine had been weakened by the explosion, and although she was at present standing up to the damage, no one could tell how much more she could stand. It was possible that if a heavy pressure of air were turned on, unseen weaknesses in the plates might give under the strain and develop into an inrush of water beyond their power to overcome.

"I was anxious to avoid using an air pressure if

possible, in case the distortion should make the leaks worse," he explained later.

So he had a man standing by ready to shut the fore end doors to isolate the compartment and to turn on the compressed air if the emergency arose. Fortunately, the pump managed to keep the water under control, although there was a second occasion when the sea started to gain the upper hand.

It became obvious by the way the *Triumph* handled that there must be a good weight of the ship missing forward. Consequently the forward bulkhead instead of the bow was withstanding the pressure of the sea. If he tried to push her along too fast this bulkhead might collapse, so the captain, with one eye on the seas, had to nurse her along, bearing in mind all the time how much pressure the bulkhead would stand. Sometimes he was unable to do more than four knots, and the highest speed attained during that nightmare journey was a little over nine knots.

Nor was this his only problem. He was wide open to the attacks of the enemy, and knew full well that if a German destroyer or other surface ship came upon him his sole chance of escape lay in diving. That was his dilemma. He was aware that the *Triumph* was in no condition to dive, or rather that she could dive without difficulty, but that there was no prospect of her ever being brought to the surface again.

He did a few calculations, made allowances so far as he could for the weight of the ship that was missing forward, jotted down the amount of buoyancy he lacked through the loss of one of the main ballast tanks, then reckoned the weight of water that would flood in when the bulkhead collapsed, as it surely would, on diving. Calmly, in the middle of the North Sea in a submarine which by some freakish chance remained afloat instead of being on the bottom, he worked out these technical points.

The answer was not cheering. If forced to dive under attack, the *Triumph* would be too heavy forward by about fifty tons, and would never be able to come up again. Unless he could find buoyancy to lift an additional fifty tons, he stood no chance if the *Triumph* submerged.

Buoyancy meant empty tanks, and he had none. There were tanks forward, just where he wanted them, but they were full of fuel oil. Normally it would have been a simple matter to blow out this oil to empty the tanks and make the *Triumph* safe if the emergency arose. But oil is one of the bugbears of the submarine commander, and many a U-boat has been sent to the bottom because it trailed a streak of oil after it from a slight leak in its fuel tanks. To avoid such a leak, and to prevent the *Triumph* leaving a trail of oil on the surface, the pipe through which the oil was pumped into the tanks had been fitted with a special cap. Until this cap was shifted the oil could not be blown out by compressed air.

This cap could only be removed from outside the boat. In those conditions, with the seas as they were, it was a task which might cost a man his life. A slip and a slight miscalculation, and the man might be washed away by the waves and drowned, for the plating of a submarine offers no sure foothold for anyone.

"We must get off the war cap to blow the forward fuel tanks. Who will volunteer?" he asked.

Quietly the Chief Engine-Room Artificer, Thomas Phillips, and Petty Officer Norwood C. F. Baker undertook the risky job. Putting on their lifebelts and rigging lifelines round their bodies, they went up on deck, and while their companions clung grimly to their lines and the seas did their best to wash the two away, they managed at last to remove the cap from the pipe.

With that problem solved and the tanks blown out, the captain of the *Triumph* felt a little easier in his mind. He still had troubles, but he had a margin of safety in hand, which is what every sensible man desires.

"If the submarine starts to dive, you must shut the fore end doors and turn on the compressed air," he told the petty officer to whom he entrusted this vital task. He gathered together the remainder of the crew. "If necessary, you must evacuate to the bridge with your lifebelts on," he instructed them.

"Aye, aye, sir!" they said calmly, and resumed their tasks.

Soon after daybreak the aircraft of Coastal Command located the *Triumph* and brought a little more relief to the mind of Lieutenant-Commander McCoy.

He was moving bravely over the waters, but he needed all the succour he could get, for his ship was sorely stricken, with the internal torpedo tubes flooded, the fore hydroplanes out of action, while among other things, the strong hull of the submarine was wrenched apart amidships. The greater part of the two torpedo tubes on the upper deck had vanished. They had been sheared away by the explosion.

The Beauforts patrolling above the *Triumph* were more than a comfort. During the morning an enemy aircraft bore down on the stricken submarine, whose captain was on the bridge. "Get below," he said to the members of his crew, and waited with his two Lewis gunners for the attack. Before it could come the Beauforts swung into action and drove the enemy away. A second time during the morning an enemy aircraft sought to attack, but was driven off by the aircraft of Coastal Command.

Then the bow waves of the destroyers were sighted, and after many hours the shattered submarine reached home safely under her own power. Privileged onlookers when they saw her in dry dock could hardly believe their eyes.

Never was a ship more aptly named, and never a commander so deserved his triumph and the Distinguished Service Cross which followed. For seventy-two days she had been at sea since the war started. Secretly she had gone out on patrol, secretly she was manoeuvred into dry dock, and it was not until two years afterward that the Admiralty permitted any mention of her thrilling escape.

"*Triumph* was fortunate to survive the explosion," was the verdict of a submarine staff officer after her thrilling return in December, 1939.

7

A CHANCE IN A MILLION

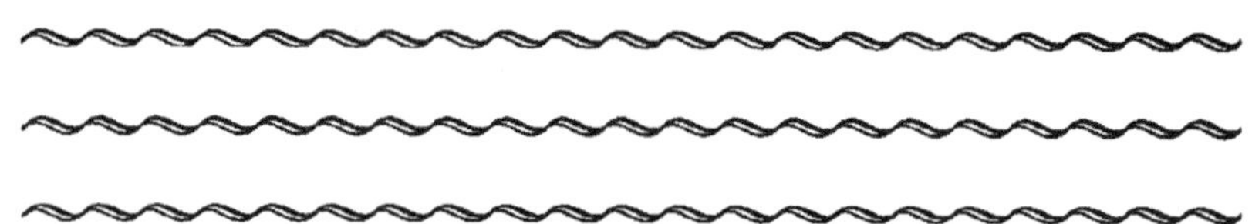

AFTER the *Triumph* came out of dry dock as good as new, her first patrol in the Mediterranean was exceptional, the sort of thing which submariners sometimes dreamed about, but were quite sure could never happen. It was on a sunny Sunday afternoon that the *Triumph* left harbour to sink enemy ships and collect such information about the sea-going habits of the enemy as could be garnered by her captain, Lieutenant-Commander W. J. W. Woods. A fruitless watch of seven hours off one cape along the enemy coast drove him to try elsewhere.

At 2 o'clock the next morning he came across a merchantman of about 3,000 tons, at which he fired torpedoes. To his chagrin he missed. His attacks brought down the hunters who chased him until it grew light and continued to trail him all day. Occassionally he pushed up the periscope to find out the position of the enemy. Then he went deeper and exercised his skill in his efforts to escape. It was 4 o'clock in the afternoon before he shook them off and could relax, after fourteen anxious hours.

For three days things went on in their uneventful ways, empty seas and no ships, while the crew watched and waited and carried out their routine duties. About 8 o'clock one night a red glow in the sky made the captain wonder if the Royal Air Force was busy in that direction, but his curiosity remained unsatisfied.

Next day it looked as though his luck would change, for he was patrolling beneath the surface about 9 o'clock in the morning when the hydrophone operator reported the sound of a ship. An examination through the periscope disclosed a merchant ship close inshore. She was a prize of about 5,000 tons, but her position made it impossible to attack her. She was, however, escorted by an armed liner of 2,000 tons and Lieutenant-Commander Woods decided to attack the escort instead. Quietly he took up position and was about to fire his torpedoes when mechanical trouble prevented him.

By the time the trouble was rectified, the chance was lost. But an hour later came a much better chance, for two merchantmen hove in sight. The captain studied them carefully through the periscope. One of the ships of 3,000 tons was fully laden, the other was in ballast. He marked the course and speed of the laden ship and noted her range while manoeuvring to attack, and when he was 2,000 yards away with the ship coming into his sights he fired his torpedoes. Unhappily the bow of the *Triumph* swung off the target as the torpedoes went away and instead of sinking the ship they exploded on the beach.

What the captain of the *Triumph* said is not recorded. One thing is certain—the failure of his attack did not deprive him of his sense of humour, although the barking and howling of a dog ashore was not particularly soothing in the circumstances.

"Heard hostile dog barking," was his comment, to which another naval officer added his quip: "It is considered that his action in refraining from opening fire on the hostile dog was correct."

Hopefully the captain of the *Triumph* continued his patrol. The next afternoon the atmosphere was so clear that it was possible to see a high mountain from a distance of 80 miles. This was adverse for submarine work, and two more days were spent in gazing at blank horizons.

Then dawned his lucky day, notwithstanding that it started disappointingly. About 7 o'clock in the morning he sighted a convoy which turned out to be four small ships, escorted by an armed liner of 5,000 tons and an anti-submarine trawler. His torpedoes were far too valuable to waste on the small ships, but the armed liner was certainly a worth-while target. He began to work into position to attack her, but she was too elusive and escaped before he could fire.

The quiet eyes at the periscope of the *Triumph*

noted a French ship being escorted by a trawler some two hours later. That vessel must have had on board something which the enemy needed badly, otherwise there would have been no escort.

Quietness reigned for the rest of the morning. Then at midday the officer of the watch sighted an aircraft approaching to attack, and the hooter sent the crew to diving stations while the *Triumph* did a crash dive.

A few minutes after 2 o'clock the unexpected began to happen, for two merchantmen were seen approaching. It needed but a glance to see that they were fully loaded, and at once the captain of the *Triumph* altered course toward the shore in order to draw in and wait for them.

The steady progress of the oncoming ships was eagerly marked through the periscope. Each was about 2,500 tons and their course made it plain to Lieutenant-Commander Woods that they were bound for a port a mile or two away. He was hopeful, but like all submarine commanders he knew there was many a slip twixt cup and lip—the disappointments which had dogged him on the patrol emphasized it. Nevertheless he could not refrain from feeling optimistic, for the ships proceeded steadily on their course while the motors of the *Triumph* drove her along until she reached a point about a mile off shore, where the captain determined to lurk.

The weather was threatening, with an overcast sky that presaged rain. He watched the ships carefully through the periscope as they slowly approached, working out their speed and distance. More than once he noted the leaden skies, saw little flurries of wind whip across the waves and wondered if the rain would hold off until he got in his attack.

Every minute brought them nearer. Every minute the skies grew darker. A few drops of rain began to fall. Then suddenly a squall of rain slashed across the face of the sea and blotted out everything. All sight of the ships was lost.

The captain of the *Triumph* waited anxiously for the squall to blow over. That deluge provided a heaven-sent chance for the ships to alter course and escape, and judging by his previous experiences on the patrol it was the sort of trick that Fate would play him. But this time Fate was kinder and he was presented with a chance in a million.

As the squall died away and the rain cleared, he picked up the two vessels again in his periscope, still steaming on the same course directly toward him. They were just under two miles away. Giving a few quiet orders, the captain of the *Triumph* started to move out toward them in a discreet circle. A few minutes later one of the ships changed course directly for the shore. The captain watched, fascinated. Then he realized that she intended to anchor right under his nose. He saw the other ship following the first.

It was almost unbelievable. The leading steamer dropped anchor and a minute or two later the other let her anchor run out just three hundred yards away. That two ships should come to anchor right in front of the submarine that was stalking them was unique, the chance that all submarine men pray for and seldom get.

Moving circumspectly until the *Triumph* was no more than 1,400 yards away, the captain fired one torpedo. It ran true. As it hit the first ship, there was a big explosion, followed by dense clouds of smoke which completely obscured both ships. For some minutes the captain of the *Triumph* could see nothing. Then the smoke dispersed and the torpedoed ship had already vanished beneath the sea, while the other ship had swung on her anchor until she was stern on to the submarine.

A ship stern on is a target that no submarine commander would willingly select. But Lieutenant-Commander Woods felt so certain that the other ship would slip her anchor and escape him by zigzagging that he determined to risk a shot. He did—and missed.

His disappointment was tempered by relief as he saw the crew of the second ship lowering a boat and pulling frantically toward the shore, which was only half a mile away. The ship was a gift to him. She lay at anchor fully laden without a soul on board to defend her, a sitting bird, if ever there was one. Closing in to within a thousand yards, Lieutenant-Commander Woods got his sights on her, aimed at the funnel and gave the order to fire a torpedo. It sped straight to the target, there was a heavy explosion and in a minute or two the ship was gone, just twenty-one minutes after the first had sunk.

The captain of the *Triumph* stole away eastward along the coast, well pleased with his afternoon's work, as well he might be, for it is not unlikely that he robbed the enemy of ships and cargo worth half a million or more. He came to the surface in the moonlight about 9 o'clock that night and twenty-four hours later received a signal which brought him safely to harbour.

Describing how his attack took place right off the shore, he commented dryly: "It is hoped, therefore, that it had some moral as well as material effect."

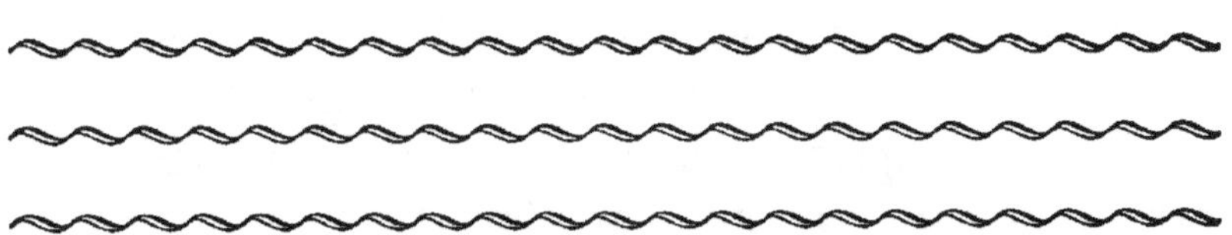

8

URSULA

HER name conjured up a religious atmosphere redolent of a saintly woman, innocent and inoffensive, gentle and meek—which goes to show how deceptive names can be, for the *Ursula* in her drab grey dress was by no means inoffensive, and any gentleness and meekness associated with her saintly name was quite illusory, as she proved to the German Naval Command. She was no ocean-going giant, but one of the coastal submarines of 540 tons, built to operate in home waters. Her speed of eleven knots on the surface, while not high, was sufficient to enable her to overtake the slower merchant ships. She was about 190 feet in length, with a crew of 31 officers and men, and as Lieutenant-Commander G. C. Phillips took the handles of the periscope in his hands in those December days to search the horizon he hungered for a chance to strike the enemy. He remembered the names of other submarines whose patrols were linked with his in a long chain, and wondered whose way the luck would run. He knew where they were, so he could get into touch with them if necessary.

On December 13th some mine-sweepers were sighted. He studied them carefully through the periscope. There were six of them in line abreast, steering to the north. Were they sweeping? The sight of minesweepers never fails to arouse the expectation of a submarine captain, for they so often preface the appearance of enemy warships. Cogitating on the question, he went his way in the opposite direction.

When darkness veiled the seas, the *Ursula* came to the surface to blow out the stale air and recharge her batteries. It was a black night, and the captain was a little uncertain of his position. Many small craft indicated that land was near.

Out of the darkness, at 8:45 p.m., flashed a light. It was the Heligoland Light which, burning for a short time, helped to fix the *Ursula's* position. It also indicated something more—that there were certain German ships at sea which needed its guidance—and in conjunction with those six trawlers in line abreast, it was some evidence of enemy activity. Ordering a sounding to be taken, Lieutenant-Commander Phillips studied the depth on his chart, and with the fix from the Heligoland Light was able to pin-point his position.

Later, after the batteries had been charged and the crew had taken a meal, the *Ursula* went warily in the direction of Heligoland. The quick eyes of the look-out and the officer of the watch stared into the darkness for a blob of denser black which meant a ship, or a faint curve which denoted a bow wave. Five times during the night the alarm brought men from their bunks as the officer of the watch sighted darkened ships, but the *Ursula* went unmolested and unseen on her way. Diving before daylight, she held her course toward the island of Heligoland, the great fortress which Germany has constructed to guard her gate from the Elbe into the North Sea.

When day came the seas were empty. For an hour or so the periscope sweeps of the horizon disclosed nothing. At 10 o'clock in the morning smoke was sighted, which developed into three destroyers and a cruiser of the *Koln* class. Quickly the captain took the range and noted their course. He was disappointed to find that the enemy ships were five miles away and steaming south, which made it impossible for him to get near enough to attack them. All he could do was to wait and watch and hope.

Nothing occurred for the next hour. But at 11.15 a.m. more smoke was sighted on the horizon. The captain stared into the periscope. "It's the same group!" he thought, as he saw the cruiser of the *Koln* class.

He started counting the destroyers. There were six, which indicated a new formation. For the time being he could not make out whether he was ahead or astern of the ships, but he believed he was astern. Altering course to make an attack, he realized at length that the ships were approaching. There were three destroyers strung out on each side of the ship to screen her from attack, and the *Ursula* was in front of the port wing of destroyers. With this strong escort it appeared that any submarine attempting to attack would surely be destroyed, for the cruiser was so closely guarded that success seemed well-nigh impossible.

Neither the fact that the odds were seven to one, nor the possibility of failure crossed the mind of Lieutenant-Commander Phillips. His one concern was how best to seize this big chance. The plan shaped in his mind, and he began to circle to the east at periscope depth. He calculated from the speed of the approaching warships that by the time he had swung round in a half-circle from the east to the west he would be able to fire his torpedoes at the cruiser, which ought to present him with nearly a broadside shot. Many an enemy ship has been missed because the bow of the submarine was just swinging off the target when the torpedoes were fired, and he was determined that he would not be cheated in this way. He planned to attack with accurately aimed shots when his bow was dead on the target and not swinging at all.

A few minutes later he ran so close to the leading destroyer that he was forced to dive deeper and pass right under her keel. Thus, with the utmost boldness and courage, he dodged the screen of destroyers and rose to firing depth inside the cruiser's guard. By the time he had run in to within 1,200 yards of the cruiser, the second destroyer had passed ahead of the *Ursula*. Sixteen minutes after sighting the warships he gave the order to fire. For the moment the noise of the torpedoes rushing through the waters drowned all other noises in the ears of the hydrophone operator.

"Torpedoes running, sir," he reported.

The captain listened anxiously and watched the seconds ticking away. Sixty seconds passed. He waited, tense. It should be about now. Seventy seconds. The sound of a tremendous explosion relieved the tension and brought a smile to his face. A few seconds later, before he had a chance to say anything, a mightier explosion on which another explosion was superimposed shook the *Ursula* and smashed her lights. It was evident that two torpedoes had struck home.

"The engine noises have ceased, sir," said the hydrophone operator. There were vast, rending, grinding, crashing noises, with great gushing sounds to denote the complete disintegration of that mass of metal which only seconds previously was a powerful cruiser. "I've never heard anything like it in my life, sir," said the amazed operator.

The firing of the torpedoes so upset the balance of the submarine that she bucketed upward and threatened to give herself away by breaking surface. But the captain got her firmly under control and forced her down again as he made to escape. Overhead the destroyers could be heard breaking their formation to search for the *Ursula*. Four of the destroyers closed in, going fast, then reducing speed and giving every indication of a pending attack. The strange thing was that these threats failed to develop into an actual attack, and the destroyers never dropped a single depthcharge. It was incomprehensible to the captain of the *Ursula* at that time, and it remains a mystery to this day. These silent attacks, as he termed them, gradually faded away to the south-west, and three-quarters of an hour after the explosion the captain took the *Ursula* up to periscope depth and looked through the periscope towards the spot between one and two miles away where he had torpedoed the cruiser. Two destroyers were on the scene, but the cruiser had vanished.

As the *Ursula* glided into base and moored beside the depot ship, it was a happy crew that crowded on her decks. In the pocket of Lieutenant-Commander G. C. Phillips were two pink official telegraph forms, one from Sir Max Horton, congratulating him and the crew on "a great achievement," and the other from the Commander-in-Chief of the Home Fleet consisting of two simple words: "Well done!"

If brevity is indeed the soul of wit, then some of the officers in the British submarine service must be the wittiest men alive, for it is said that they never write two words when one will do—a terseness that is preferred by the staff officers, because it gives a clearer picture of operations than a verbose account can do. But there was one submarine commander who excelled himself and all others in the service by condensing into six lines all the incidents of a fortnight's patrol.

This feat was too much for one of the staff who, much as he preferred words to be used sparingly, was stung into retorting that it overstepped the mark for brevity. Which seems to indicate that brevity can be carried too far even in the silent service, and that one officer at least does not wish the Navy to grow quite dumb!

The Scots do their best to maintain a mistaken reputation for having no sense of humour by thinking out jokes against themselves which send chuckles round the world. Lieutenant A. J. Mackenzie, who later took the *Ursula* out to do as much damage as possible to enemy shipping, evidently played cricket and had a sense of humour to boot. Diving just before 6 o'clock next morning, he went steadily ahead on his motors for hour after hour.

The sun shone. The sea was like glass. Conditions for a submarine attack were as bad as they could be. Scanning the enemy shore he saw a merchant ship aground. She was not aground when he had prowled along there during a previous patrol, and whether she had been driven ashore by Allied submarines, surface ships or aircraft, the Axis were robbed of a ship of 5,000 tons, a ship that had undoubtedly been stealing across the channel from Sicily to Libya.

Regretting that she was not about to steam into

his sights, he went his way, wondering whether he would be lucky enough to fall in with any ships engaged in supplying the enemy forces in Libya.

Two hours later, just after 3 o'clock, he swung the periscope calmly enough to all appearances, but with no little excitement in his mind, upon a cloud of smoke which turned out to be a convoy. Speeding up in the direction of the target, he raised the periscope now and again until he made out a fully-loaded troopship and a merchant ship in ballast, with an escort of three Italian torpedo-boats. Hunting through his reference books, he managed to identify the transport and merchantman as vessels of 9,600 tons.

There was no cover of any sort for him, not a ripple on the sea to blend with the ripples of his periscope to confuse the enemy when he raised it for momentary glimpses. There were no clouds in the sky to cast shadows on the water to mask his movements. The young Scotsman, however, was not without guile. His clever brain planned to take advantage of these seemingly hopeless conditions to cover his attack. As the sun shone brazenly in the sky and cast a fierce glare over the sea, he determined to strike with the sun right behind him, using the path of light on the sea as a guide to his target, and hoping that the glare would dazzle the eyes of the enemy look-outs and hide the tracks of his torpedoes.

It was a triumph of tactics which fulfilled all his hopes. Just after 4 o'clock, a few minutes less than an hour after sighting the ships, he attained his firing position and sent away his torpedoes at the loaded transport, which he selected as his target. Altering course at top speed to get away from his firing position, he went deeper, listening anxiously, wondering whether he had succeeded or failed, whether his judgment was going to be justified. He stood there, straining his ears, watching the hydrophone operator, whose report that the torpedoes were running brought him comfort and hope. It seemed a very long time, but was actually 1 minute and 43 seconds, before a big explosion told him that one torpedo at least had scored a hit, and that his tactics had triumphed.

A few minutes later things began to grow lively for the *Ursula*. Depth-charges began to drop astern. Ten exploded one after the other, each a little closer than the last. There was no doubt that the hunters were on the track of the submarine. Stopping the gyroscope and the generator and working the hydroplanes by hand instead of motor, he cut down speed to a crawl to reduce the sounds in the boat. Lights were broken, but he still kept the fans working to circulate the air.

Twenty minutes later he slid slowly up to periscope depth to take a quick look. The transport had stopped. His practised eye saw that she was lower in the water, sinking on an even keel. The four lifeboats, which were swung out before he fired the torpedoes, had been launched and were standing away from the ship. The merchantman in ballast was fouling the heavens with smoke as it steamed away to the south as hard as it could go. One of the torpedo boats was about a mile away searching for the *Ursula*; the other two were busy by the transport picking up survivors.

Well satisfied with his afternoon's work, Lieutenant Mackenzie dived lower and continued to move slowly from the scene, while the crew busied themselves in rectifying the damage. They had not escaped entirely. Some of the depth-charges had been close enough to break a number of lamps in the after part of the submarine; one or two of the voice-pipes had been fractured, a ventilator from the batteries was damaged, and one or two bits of glass smashed. It was nothing much, just enough to make the captain feel thankful that the depth-charges were not nearer.

Once when he used the telemotor to raise the periscope he saw the torpedo boat move directly toward him as it picked up the sound. It confirmed his judgment in not using the ballast pumps to alter the trim of the submarine. Instead, he practised a trick which was not uncommon in the last war—selecting one or two big stokers, he made them move forward after firing the torpedoes in order to lighten the stern and push the bow down, and he was able by moving these living counter-weights to adjust the trim of the *Ursula* as he desired without running the risk of using the ballast pumps at all. It discloses how delicately a submarine must be trimmed if she is to do what her captain desires.

Some forty minutes after making his examination of the transport he ascended again and raised the periscope. To the south in the dusk he saw the transport all but under. Her decks were awash. She was down by the stern, although she still remained on an even keel. He watched patiently until the deepening dusk flung a curtain over the scene and prevented him from seeing her take the last plunge.

"Bad light stopped play," was his subtle comment, which the Italians, who do not play cricket, would fail to understand.

After charging his batteries that night, he trimmed down the ship, stopped the engines and floated on the surface till dawn. His look-outs on the darkest nights when there was no moon could pick up a small ship without lights at a distance of over two miles, and the crew of the *Ursula* were so well trained a team that they could dive from this stopped position in thirty-five seconds.

On that occasion luck was with the *Ursula*. But there were exasperating moments when it was otherwise. About 3.30 one afternoon her captain sighted two fine prizes in the shape of a motor vessel of 10,000 tons and another of 3,000 tons some 4,000 yards away. He gave his orders to prepare the torpedoes while he worked into position to attack them off a prominent cape. The motor vessels were travelling at ten knots on a course which took them close in to the land.

For an hour he manœuvred the *Ursula* into the ideal attacking position. He took a last swift look. The range was 2,000 yards as he ordered a salvo of torpedoes to be fired.

At that very moment the merchantmen altered course! They did not know he was there nor realize how closely they had escaped destruction.

All his endeavours were frustrated because he had selected the exact spot and moment when all enemy ships passing that way altered course to round the point. Anyone would have sworn that the ships running the gauntlet from Italy would hold on until they were nearer land before changing helm to hug the coast, but they did not. His disappointment at seeing his prizes slip from his grasp needs no stressing.

That is typical of the submarine captain's lot. He may wait weeks or months for a chance. For every success there are so many disappointments, owing to tricks of circumstance and sea and weather and human fallibility, that only a man of unshakable physical and moral courage, with tremendous patience and faith in himself, his crew and his ship can expect to make his mark.

9

TRIUMPHS OF

THE *CACHALOT*

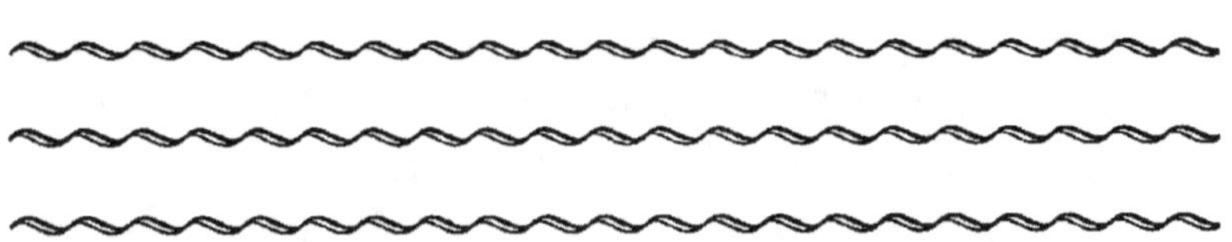

Two of the foremost inventors who helped to develop the submarine from a crude invention into a potent weapon of destruction were the Americans John P. Holland and Simon Lake, both of whom in their day donned the mantle of the prophets. "Submarines could not fight submarines," said Holland long years ago.

"This simple fact makes submarines so potent that I believe they will be able to enforce peace between maritime nations," wrote Simon Lake. "How can one ward off an attack from the unseen? Dreadnaughts may be pitted against dreadnaughts; aeroplanes against dirigible, gun against gun, man against man; but take away sight and all becomes chaos. In this lies the superiority of the submarine, since human vision is incapable of penetrating through the water except for a distance of a very few feet."

Simon Lake was possessed of foresight; he not only called attention to the fact that sound waves were carried to submarines under water, but he even invented a receiver for locating the direction of the sound, yet he was apparently so obsessed by the sounds given off by surface ships that he failed to realize that the sounds of a submarine moving under water might also be heard, and that ears might one day take the place of eyes and enable an unseen submarine to be attacked and destroyed by the use of sound locators of a delicacy then undreamed of.

Twice within thirty-four days Lieutenant-Commander J. D. Luce proved the fallacy of Holland's contention by attacking and sinking a U-boat. *Cachalot* left her base one day during 1940, to carry out the special mission of laying a minefield where it was likely to do the enemy most harm. The *Cachalot* was primarily a mine-layer, built specially for the task, and she carried a large number of mines for covering a considerable area. In addition she was armed with torpedo tubes and a gun so that she could serve the dual purpose of laying mines and attacking shipping.

Generally known in the service as "eggs," these mines were stowed in the casing on top of the pressure hull, along which they ran on rails that were curved downward clear of the stern of the boat. An endless chain, operated by a shaft from inside the mining compartment of the boat, hooked up underneath each mine and carried it along the rails until it came to the downward curve when it slipped off the hook on the chain and dropped astern into the sea. Set for the requisite depth before the submarine left port, the mines were the particular charge of the mining torpedo gunner's mate, known for short as the "Mining T.I.," otherwise the torpedo instructor, who had been specially trained to deal with them. During the laying of a minefield, he controlled the endless chain and by varying its speed he could vary the distance apart at which the mines were laid, in the same way that an alteration in the speed of the *Cachalot* would also vary the distance between the mines. For instance, if the chain worked quickly and the *Cachalot* moved slowly, the mines fell into the sea close together, whereas if the chain worked slowly and the *Cachalot* moved at high speed the mines fell into the sea much further apart, because the submarine covered a greater distance in the time that the mines took to glide along the deck of the submarine and drop over the stern.

Mines are very weighty and a submarine could not dispose of dozens of them without seriously interfering with her trim, consequently some compensation has to be made for this loss of weight. It is the special duty of the mining engine-room artificer, otherwise "Mining E.R.A.", to attend to this. As the mines are laid he stands by to flood the tanks with additional water to make up the weight and prevent the submarine from losing trim.

Where each mine is laid is indicated on the chart, and if an enemy ship gets into trouble just there, the

Admiralty and the captain of the mine-layer have a shrewd idea of the cause, even if the Germans are left in doubt.

As absolute secrecy must govern the laying of a minefield, the captain of a mine-layer is compelled to seize an opportunity when no shipping is about and do the job as quickly as possible, for it is imperative for the submarine to "lay its eggs" and depart without the enemy being any the wiser.

There was an occasion however, when things did not go normally. The *Cachalot* was caught in a heavy gale. Lieutenant-Commander Luce heard the mines crashing about above his head in the casing. Crash! went a mine on the starboard side. Bang! went a mine on the port casing. It sounded evil. Between whiles they creaked like an inn sign in a high wind. It was most alarming. They bumped and crashed together until the *Cachalot* was in grave danger of being blown to pieces by one of her own mines, although no one on board realized how close they were to disaster.

When the seas quietened, it became possible to examine the deadly cargo. One mine had been flung about with such force that three of its horns were damaged. The mine was designed so that when it was laid a touch on one horn would blow a ship to pieces. This mine had crashed against three of its horns and damaged them, but fortunately the mooring rope was not jerked by these movements and the mine remained safe. Some beneficent spirit was certainly watching over the *Cachalot* and her crew at that moment.

Without fuss and ignoring the risk, the "Mining T.I." got down among the mines to see what had happened. It was a nasty job, moving about in water up to his chest among these giant black spheres of death. Having dealt with the damaged mine by withdrawing the detonator, he discovered one from which the sinker had broken loose: how it had managed to break loose without pulling on the mooring rope and exploding the mine is a mystery. He was thus able to avert another grave risk, for there was the likelihood that as the train of mines moved aft it would have become alive in leaving the *Cachalot* and would probably have blown her stern off and involved them in a terrible catastrophe. With the cold winter seas surging about him, he obviated these dangers and the mines were duly laid, while the crew of the submarine carried on as though it were commonplace to knock the horns of a mine and bend them! They were a gallant crew.

To revert to 1940, Lieutenant-Commander Luce, having successfully laid his mines, stole quietly away. There was a stiff breeze of about 25 knots, and a fairish sea, with a bright moon that made it possible to see for miles. The weather had been bad all day, but a change in the wind blew the rain away and brought a lovely clear night. The crew were fed, the batteries charged and the *Cachalot* moved steadily along on the surface with a following sea and wind.

About one o'clock in the early morning the captain went up on the bridge to have a look round, as he had done many a time before during his career in the submarine service. Upon the surface of the sea the moon laid a silver path along which the *Cachalot* steered. The night was very beautiful. For ten minutes the captain stood on the bridge chatting with the officer of the watch. "I'm going below now," he said, and turned away.

"Object on the starboard bow, sir," sang out the starboard look-out at that instant.

They had seen so many fishing craft during the night that the captain thought it was probably another. Focusing his binoculars, he examined it carefully. He grew taut. It did not look like a fishing vessel.

At his quick touch the night alarm bell rang through the boat to call the crew to diving stations. The tall figure of the captain in sea boots, grey flannels and sweater, stood there in the moonlight gazing intently through his binoculars. It was a U-boat, about four miles away, steering right across the bows of the *Cachalot*. No need for him to work into position. The U-Boat was doing that for herself.

"Go below," he ordered the officer of the watch and the three look-outs, who disappeared through the hatch. He stood there with the signalman, waiting anxiously for the report that the tubes were ready. He was all keyed up, as he estimated the course and speed of the enemy.

"I'm going to fire torpedoes," he instructed the torpedo officer. "Bring the tubes to the ready."

He waited impatiently, wondering how much longer they were going to be. His tension was so great that it seemed about three-quarters of an hour before the tubes were ready; but it was only a few minutes from the time the enemy was first sighted. Fixing the glasses in the night sight, he stood, watching intently for the U-boat to move into position.

"Stand by—fire!" he ordered, and the torpedoes sped on their way. "Press the hooter," he said to the signalman beside him, and followed the latter through the hatchway, closed the hatch as the water began to flood through the Kingston valves into the ballast tanks, to take the *Cachalot* under. Just as he got to the bottom of the conning-tower, seventy seconds after firing the torpedoes, he heard an explosion.

"Propeller noises have ceased, sir," reported the hydrophone operator, who detected the sound of engines right up to the moment of the explosion.

Putting on the headphones, the captain listened, but heard nothing. Ordering two tubes to be reloaded, he brought the *Cachalot* to the surface and steered toward the position in which he had last seen the U-boat. Two miles away, showing up quite clearly in the moonlight, a heavy black mass, about half a mile in diameter, was lying on the surface of the sea. Around it in all directions the seas were breaking with white caps, but within that patch was nothing but a sullen, oily swell. The men in the U-boat had gone to their doom leaving only that blot on the seas to mark their tomb. Slowly the *Cachalot* explored that patch of oil for survivors, but there was none. The air was foetid with oily fumes; the thick oil clung tenaciously to the plates of the *Cachalot* until she dived at dawn and washed the foulness away.

So Lieutenant-Commander Luce won the D.S.O. and a congratulatory pink telegram from the Admiral of Submarines.

"It was frightfully simple. I did not have to alter course at all," he said afterwards. "Of course, I was very excited at the time."

This submarine officer had the experience in 1936 of being captured by Chinese pirates when he was on the China station. He was returning with another submarine officer from Pekin, where he had been on leave, when the pirates swooped down and took him and his companion prisoner. For three days they were held until the Commander-in-Chief of the China station heard of their plight. Then an aircraft from the aircraft carrier *Eagle* became so threatening that the pirates concluded that it would be wiser to release their prisoners, which they did.

How many minefields the *Cachalot* has laid in the war is known to the Admiralty. There was an occasion when Commander Luce waited breathlessly while he watched a ship run right into one of his minefields and pass safely through without striking a mine. "I watched her hopefully as she steamed over *Cachalot's* previous minefield, and was disappointed to see her go clear," he commented afterwards.

In his earlier command, the *Rainbow*, he operated in zones so frigid that it was necessary to keep a man continually at work chipping the ice away from the rim of the hatchway in order that the hatch could be tightly closed to allow the submarine to dive safely if the emergency arose. Many a time he stood upon the bridge until the drenching spray froze his clothes so hard and solid that it was impossible for him to discard them unaided when he got below. It was as though he had been encased in plaster of paris and he was compelled to get a member of the crew to help him to struggle out of them. Many a time after his sea-boots were tugged off he donned his bedroom slippers and wore them all day until the time came at night for him to go up on the bridge.

Sometimes the temperature inside the boat dropped to 14° F., or eighteen degrees of frost. The men were compelled to pile on socks and sweaters one over the other in their endeavours to keep warm. Everything was wet and cold, conditions were very unpleasant, yet they went about their duties as cheerfully as of yore. The captain whiled away the time with a game of cribbage: "Fifteen two, fifteen four, and a pair's six, a run of four makes ten, and one for his nob!" you might hear him say, while members of the crew had desperate battles over ludo, which is known throughout the service as "uckers." The majority stowed their razors against the day they returned to port and let their beards grow. Daily their faces became hairier and more unkempt, but their cheerful spirit remained unaltered.

On other patrols it was so hot that the crew moved about inside the boat with only a towel wrapped round their middles and in their hands a "sweat rag," with which they mopped the sweat from their gleaming bodies and faces. After enduring such insufferable conditions all day, there was a natural tendency to go up on deck at night in the nude in order to cool off. But the captain in his wisdom knew that to emerge from the torrid heat into the cool night air without clothing was to court chills and pneumonia, so he kept a strict watch on the crew and saw that they put on some clothing before they went on deck.

On another occasion the *Cachalot* started off to lay another batch of "eggs" and duly completed the task. Enemy aircraft were troublesome, and four trawlers seemed bent on hunting the *Cachalot*, so her captain very discreetly moved out of the area and went off to see if he could find any U-boats making for home.

Some days later, the pilot of an aircraft happened to glance down and see a U-boat making for France. It was a chance the captains of flying boats pray for. He had, however, no bombs, but he knew what to do and did it promptly. Fixing the position, he sent off a signal which was noted in the appropriate quarters and eventually reached the *Cachalot*. Glancing at the position where the enemy was seen, Lieutenant-Commander Luce made a few notes, and found that the U-boat was about twenty-five miles away. Increasing speed, and diving well below periscope depth to avoid being sighted, he set a course toward the U-boat to try to intercept it.

Some three hours later the hydrophone operator, Telegraphist Smith, heard faint sounds in his earphones: "Something on the port quarter, sir," he reported. The sounds were barely audible and he could not identify them with certainty.

Coming up to periscope depth, the captain swung the periscope in the fading light, but there was nothing in sight. Diving deeper, he went ahead full speed on the motors for twenty minutes, then slowed down, raised the periscope and looked around. Again he saw nothing.

He was very disappointed. Going deeper, he did another burst at full speed for about ten minutes. Night was coming and he was very afraid that it might grow too dark before he could locate the enemy.

"Sounds are faint, sir," reported the hydrophone operator at 5.27 p.m. The captain steered the *Cachalot* up to thirty feet and searched with the periscope. Not a thing could he see, so he took her up to twenty feet and made another search. Moving the periscope round from port to starboard, he suddenly saw, sitting on the water, what appeared to be a little box. It was the U-boat he had been seeking plainly discernible against the horizon. She was a long way off, and he closed her at high speed while he made his calculations for firing the torpedoes. She was still about four miles away and seemed an almost impossible shot as she loomed up in his sights and he gave the order to fire.

Away went the torpedoes, and down went the *Cachalot* to about 60 feet. Commander Luce thought the explosion would never come, felt quite sure he had missed, that it was impossible to hit so small a target at that distance. He waited a lifetime—exactly five minutes—before he heard the longed-for explosion. Fifteen seconds later followed a second explosion.

So well and truly did he make his calculations and aim his torpedoes that two of them found the mark. The impossible shot was accomplished. The crew were delighted. Indeed, one of the ratings so far forgot discipline as to pat the captain on the back and say: "That was a very good shot, sir."

Being well in the danger area, the captain remained down until it was quite dark. Then he came to the surface. It was a foul night, pitch black and raining hard, so bad that he could not see for more than a hundred yards. Altering course, he steered the *Cachalot* over to the position where the U-boat had been until the well-known smell of fuel oil told him he was on the spot. For a time he cruised around. There was nothing to be heard or seen.

"Draw a bucket of water," he ordered. A bucket was dropped over the side and taken down to the control room. Upon its surface was the film of oil, which told him he had found the mark and sent another crew of German raiders to their doom.

For his skill in picking up the sounds of the U-boat and thus making a successful attack possible, Leading-Telegraphist Smith was awarded the D.S.M.

While the *Cachalot* was speeding on her way back to England, the wireless operator wrote down a message on his pad for the captain, who is now Commander J. D. Luce, D.S.O. It was a second signal of congratulation from Admiral Sir Max Horton.

10

THE EXPLOITS

OF THE *TIGRIS*

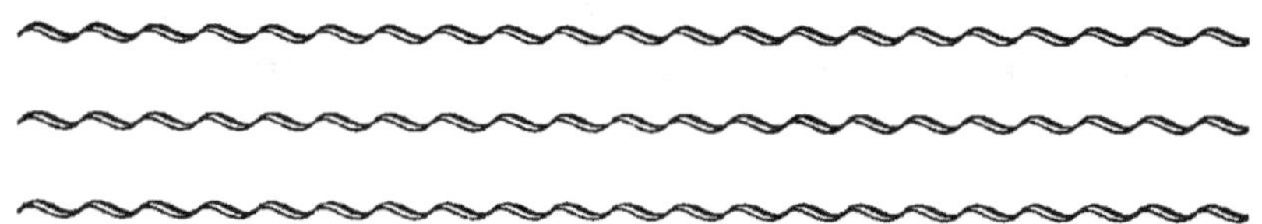

FEW men in the British submarine service have more successes to their credit than Commander Howard Francis Bone who, like many another man in the silent service, prefers actions to words. He has made the name of the *Tigris* feared in enemy circles and has achieved the distinction of sinking three U-boats in addition to eleven ships with an aggregate displacement of 38,500 tons, for which outstanding feats he has been awarded the D.S.O. and Bar and the D.S.C. and Bar.

A good story ran round the ward-rooms soon after he won the D.S.O. Returning from another patrol in which he had scored further successes, he touched at the stations of two or three other flotillas on the way back and at each was congratulated on his D.S.C. A little puzzled, he was too modest and polite to mention the error. Each time he thanked his comrades, but as it went on and he got back to base he became rather tired of the mistake.

Directly he secured alongside his depot ship, an officer leaned over the rail and shouted down to him: "Congratulations on your D.S.C.!"

"Thank you," said Bone, dryly. As soon as the two met on the quarter deck, the officer gripped him by the hand and repeated, with whole-hearted enthusiasm: "Congratulations on your D.S.C.!"

Commander Bone faced him with the ribbon of the D.S.O. on his breast. "Hang it all," he thought. "He ought to know the difference between the ribbon of the D.S.O. and the D.S.C."

"I'm delighted," said the officer.

"Thanks very much," said Commander Bone, giving the ribbon on his chest an emphatic dig with his finger. "But it isn't the D.S.C., it's the D.S.O."

For a moment the other seemed rather nonplussed, then a look of comprehension dawned in his eyes: "But didn't you know?" he enquired.

"Know what?" asked Commander Bone.

"You've been awarded the D.S.C. It was announced in the *Gazette* this morning."

The name of Bone has become famous in art and literature. Commander Bone, who comes of another branch of the same family, has now made it famous in submarine warfare. It was at Chatham, the birthplace of many a famous ship in the Royal Navy, that Commander Bone first saw the light of day on

October 20, 1908. At the age of fourteen he went to Dartmouth, to pass out into the Royal Navy in 1925. He is well built, of medium height, exactly 5 feet 8½ inches tall, with a fresh complexion, dark brown hair, a strong nose and blue eyes that look very straight at a man. Those eyes appear very stern on occasions, and his words can be to the point. But at other times his eyes twinkle merrily, particularly when he is telling a joke against himself.

The *Tigris* herself was built at Chatham, and he supervised her fitting out before taking her on her first patrol in July, 1940. His orders were to sink any ships of Hitler's invasion fleet which sailed from France, but as the invasion fleet remained in port he came back empty-handed.

His first U-boat, which fell to a torpedo during his second patrol, was vanquished by a snap attack when he shot at sight and destroyed the enemy owing to a remarkable combination of acute observation, quick action, and quicker thinking. There was no time to procrastinate. The attack was all over in three minutes.

The night was rather hazy, with a glassy sea, as the *Tigris* steamed upon the surface just after 10 o'clock. It was possible to see eight miles, and one thing they saw, which Commander Bone did not like, was a German E-boat speeding in the distance.

After sighting this craft, Commander Bone altered helm and the *Tigris* started to swing to port. As she did so Lieutenant Bennington, D.S.C., the officer of the watch, opened his eyes in amazement. An instant later Commander Bone opened his eyes, too, and both men turned and shouted to each other: "My God! A U-boat!"

The enemy was but 500 yards away, steering from port to starboard across the bows of the British submarine.

The captain's reactions were instantaneous. Reversing the rudder to hard-a-starboard, he sounded the alarm. The crew leapt to diving stations. A look-out on the bridge jumped for the conning-tower and vanished. By the time the bow of the *Tigris* was beginning to swing back to overtake the U-boat, the enemy had sighted the British submarine and started to dive.

The captain of the *Tigris* was so busy giving orders and navigating that he momentarily lost sight of her. Not so Lieutenant Bennington. His quick eyes noted that as the enemy dived she was turning to starboard. So close was the enemy half a minute previously, that Commander Bone felt sure there would be a collision. Lieutenant Bennington's observation sealed the doom of the U-boat. If she had dived first and altered helm afterwards she might have escaped, but that glimpse of her changing course as she went under gave away her position.

"He altered the starboard as he dived!" shouted the first lieutenant.

"Something had to be done quickly to catch him

before he went under," commented Commander Bone afterwards.

At that instant he judged it just possible to get the U-boat with the starboard tube of the *Tigris*. He felt sure the enemy would escape before he could bring his bow tubes to bear. It is interesting to note that the torpedo from the starboard tube travels about a hundred yards at right angles to the boat under the initial impulse of firing and then comes under the control of the gyroscope, which steers it round until it travels parallel with the torpedoes from the bow tubes. Thus a torpedo, by clever manipulation, can be made to turn corners, and if the target is just stealing across the tracks of the bow tubes out of range, it may still be possible by firing the starboard tube to catch the enemy, providing the captain thinks quickly and acts promptly.

Commander Bone did both. The men at the tubes excelled themselves. The torpedoes were ready. He issued orders and the starboard torpedo hissed through the sea.

There was a short pause of fifteen seconds. The Hun, seeking to escape, ran into the torpedo. A tremendous explosion shook the *Tigris*, and Commander Bone saw an enormous red glow light the sea. It marked the utter destruction of the U-boat, which could not have been more than 250 yards away.

Commander Bone did not wait. Fishing craft and an E-boat were in the vicinity. He saw the nearest fishing boat slip her nets and beetle off as fast as she could. Then he rang down for full speed and withdrew as quickly as possible.

Giving the Diesel engines full power, the engineer officer stepped into the control room to look at the depth gauges. They stood at 70 feet. To his startled eyes they denoted that the *Tigris* was already 70 feet below the surface and that water must be pouring into the boat to mark their own end. He turned slickly back to the engine-room. The engines were still runnning normally. It was strange. He knew they could not do that beneath the surface. Then it dawned on him that the explosion had upset the depth gauges of the *Tigris*. But it gave the engineer officer a nasty moment.

If Commander Bone demanded a very high standard of his crew, he was quick to give praise where it was due. "Success was only made possible by the excellent and cool judgment of Lieutenant Bennington," he commented on his return. "A.B. Scott deserves mention. He was look-out on the bridge at the time and scarcely touched a rung on his way to his action station and brought his tubes to the ready within a few seconds."

That success was a triumph of team work.

On another occasion he decided to dive. The faint touch of dawn was creeping across the horizon to the east as he took her down. It was too light to remain longer on the surface, and too dark to see through the periscope, so he levelled out and went ahead at two or three knots.

Just before 7 o'clock, when it was light enough to see, he raised the periscope to keep watch. The day was still and hazy. Within five minutes he saw a sight which has fallen to the lot of few submarine captains. Within range of his periscope, between four and five miles away, loomed not one U-boat, nor two U-boats, but three U-boats. The most optimistic submariners would never expect to see anything like it.

"Were you surprised?" he was once asked.

"No, I rather expected it," he said simply.

They were following each other in line ahead, and even as he picked them up in the morning mist the leader went by and passed out of range. Immediately he decided to attack the second and third.

At his signal the crew stood ready. A few terse orders sent the *Tigris* on a new course to bring him to the attacking position. He waited as patiently as he could, outwardly calm, but inwardly excited, while he closed the range and noted the course and speed of the enemy.

Up went his periscope for another look, which instantly shattered his fine plan of sinking two U-boats together. He saw two escort vessels loom up at high speed and turn straight toward the *Tigris*. For a couple of minutes he considered what to do. The way in which the escorts changed course was a clear indication that his presence was detected and that they were on his track. To persist in his attempt to destroy the two enemy submarines might endanger his own boat and lead to both enemies escaping.

Prudence and common sense dictated a change of plan. One U-boat was better than none.

"I decided to attack the third U-boat and make sure of it," he said, on his return.

When his target was within a mile and a half he fired his torpedoes and at once dived lower and altered course to escape the attack of the escorts.

"I still hadn't got used to waiting for the bang. It seemed to be an awful long time. I thought I'd missed," he once remarked.

During an attack he used to become so worked up that he gave a running commentary without being aware of it. Usually he was pessimistic. "I've missed her! I've missed her!" he would say, and at that the men in the control room smiled at each other and felt easier in their minds, for it generally meant a hit. At such moments his mental processes were so quickened that each second seemed like an hour, and in his imagination the torpedoes had already swept past the target long before they had actually reached her. Then the bang would come. "We've got her—we've got her all right!" he would exclaim.

During the attack on his second U-boat he waited for the bang of his torpedoes a few seconds more than two minutes. After two explosions he risked a quick look. A lot of brown smoke was drifting up into the sky. Two U-boats rode the seas. The third had vanished. Those shots were a fine tribute to his skill in estimating the distance, for the running times of the torpedoes indicated a range of only a few yards more than his estimate.

For half an hour the crew of the *Tigris* had an exciting time as the depth charges exploded about them. In thirty-seven minutes they counted eleven, but luckily the hunters careered about all over the place and missed them.

Making his way steadily out to sea, Commander Bone in due course reported his success and so shared with Commander Luce of the *Cachalot* the honour of having destroyed two U-boats. After that attack he got mixed up with a big fishing fleet at midnight and was dodging about for hours until dawn before he finally won free; it was a worrying time.

Hunting just off the French coast in the early morning during another patrol he sighted a laden tanker of 1,500 tons in the bright moonlight just before 5 o'clock. It was about three miles away and burned dim lights in the bows. Stealing up to within a mile and a half, Commander Bone waited for her to come into his sights. Firing his torpedoes, he watched one hit amidships. A great column of water rose into the air, gleaming like a gigantic fountain in the moonbeams. When the fountain subsided the tanker was gone.

Bad weather hit the *Tigris* with a vengeance. The wind increased. The seas rose until conditions on board became so uncomfortable that Commander Bone was forced to heave to. Seeking protection from the tempest, he took the boat down to 90 feet. He found little mitigation. The surging action of the giant seas reached down and swung the *Tigris* about like a pendulum. Lower still he steered the *Tigris* for another 60 feet. Even here, 150 feet beneath the surface, her movements were so violent that the fiddles had to be fixed to prevent the crockery from being flung off the ward-room table and smashed to pieces.

The gale was the fiercest that Spain had experienced for 140 years. In the mouth of the Tagus sixteen ships were blown ashore. An immense fire, fanned by the gale, developed in Bilbao, while a train was blown bodily off a railway bridge at Santander.

Yet the *Tigris* survived. For five days that little band of men, immured for long hours in their steel tube, suffered the worst of gales. Still they remained cheerful. If the gale imposed conditions upon them that were barely tolerable, they had at least one thing to thank it for. During it, Commander Bone managed to torpedo another ship, but found it impossible to close the cap of one of the torpedo tubes afterwards. Something was jammed in it. What it was, they had no means of knowing. For a couple of hours they struggled to close the cap. Then the rough seas washed away the obstruction, so the tail end of the gale did them a good turn.

Later another gale hit the *Tigris*. Just when it was at its height, about 10.30 at night, the officer of the watch, Lieutenant M. H. Jupp, D.S.C., sighted a darkened ship which turned out to be a big tanker of 10,000 or 12,000 tons. At once he turned to attack her, while warning the captain of her presence. Commander Bone conned the tanker. She was a rich prize, worth more than gold to the enemy.

Twelve minutes after she was sighted, he fired his torpedoes at her. To his chagrin he saw her alter course about half a minute after he fired, and his torpedoes missed. Three minutes later he fired more torpedoes, but the tanker steamed serenely on. Those great seas which made the *Tigris* stagger and roll could not fail to affect the comparatively puny torpedoes, which weighed less than two tons each.

"I had spent so much money on him I couldn't afford to let him go, so I dragged up the gun's crew and manned the gun, although the platform was very wet and unstable," he said.

Signalling for full speed, he raced after her until he reduced the distance between them to half a mile. The tanker seemed unaware of the presence of the *Tigris*. Her look-outs must have been half asleep.

They were soon shaken up by the high explosive shells from the 4-inch gun of the submarine which found the target at once. The tanker fought back and for nearly two hours the submarine and tanker were engaged in a desperate battle. Both ships used flashless powder which made it difficult to locate the guns that were firing, but the gunners of the *Tigris* managed at last to silence the guns of the tanker.

Four times the tanker attempted to ram the *Tigris* and four times the deft seamanship of Commander

Bone evaded the attacks and closed the range to give his gunners a chance. At least ten shells penetrated the starboard side of the tanker below the water line. Oil began to spread far and wide over the sea.

Then the British gunners scored three hits astern which made the tanker list heavily. Steering right in, Commander Bone allowed his gunners to pump shells into her. The guns of the tanker were silent. Her screws ceased to turn. She lay still in a great black patch in which the white-crested seas were subdued by the oil pouring out of the riddled tanks. To Commander Bone's surprise, she did not take fire and she seemed to be a long time sinking.

His first lieutenant happened in peace time to be a British tanker captain, so Commander Bone called him up to the bridge. "She's a long time sinking," he said.

"Where have you hit her?" asked the first lieutenant.

Commander Bone told him.

The first lieutenant, with his expert knowledge of tankers, laughed. "That's quite enough. She'll sink all right," he said.

But to make quite sure, Commander Bone drew off to deal the death blow. Just before midnight a torpedo hit the sinking tanker amidships. Knowing that the gunfire would soon bring patrols to the spot, the captain of the *Tigris* steered rapidly from the scene.

A day or two earlier he had managed to pick up

some Frenchmen, who very enthusiastically handed up the shells for the gun. When it came to firing the torpedo Commander Bone decided to send them back to their bunks. The shock of the torpedo exploding knocked down a clock which hit one of the Frenchmen on the head and a few moments later their officer appeared to tell them that the captain had torpedoed the tanker.

"And me also!" added the Frenchman ruefully, rubbing his head.

Two nights later Commander Bone picked up two of the strangest-looking individuals who ever put to sea in small boats. They were both dressed in smart black felt hats and fashionable overcoats, while each carried an attache case and an umbrella. What they were doing in that garb at that time, they alone knew, but they rowed toward the submarine for dear life. Unfortunately when they got alongside, the seas upset their craft and they lost their attache cases and umbrellas. But the crew of the *Tigris* managed to drag them on board, very wet and very happy to be rescued. Who they were and what they were doing must remain undisclosed until the war is over.

The next day the captain of the *Tigris* lay off Brest, hoping to deal a deadly blow at the *Scharnhorst* and *Gneisenau.* The trap was set for the much-bombed ships, but they failed to come out, and the Royal Air Force confined them there for months, until their dramatic escape through the English Channel back to Germany. Later on, like other captains of submarines, Commander Bone set off to try to intercept the *Bismarck*, but he had been speeding on the surface only an hour when he happened to listen in to the 1 o'clock news and learned that the *Bismarck* had already been sunk.

He met with every imaginable kind of weather from a flat calm to a tempest during his patrols, and the atmospheric conditions were sometimes almost incredible, with quite abnormal visibility. Once, for instance, he caught sight of a torpedo-boat approaching the *Tigris* at full speed and wasted no time in diving. Unable to understand why the hydrophone operator could not hear the vessel and why no attack was made, he steered up to periscope depth to look round. To his surprise there was no boat in sight. What he mistook for a torpedo boat was actually a headland forty miles away, but owing to the refraction—the bending of the rays of light by the peculiar atmospheric conditions—the headland was distorted into the appearance of a torpedo-boat. It completely bluffed him.

At other times he saw lighthouses behave as if they were no longer subject to natural laws. He was looking at a lighthouse one day when suddenly it disappeared as though at the touch of a magician. Five minutes later he was staring at the same spot when it reappeared. Another time a lighthouse appeared as three images in a vertical line, two were the right way up and one was upside down. More mystifying still inasmuch as they seemed to defy the laws of refraction were the three lighthouses he saw standing side by side. Refracted images usually appear in a vertical line above or below the real object and are normally caused by horizontal layers in the atmosphere. But the extraordinary phenomenon seen by Commander Bone on this occasion was apparently caused by vertical layers or pillars in the atmosphere which were probably formed by the updraughts brought about by the configuration of the land. More than once he saw a lighthouse with an inverted image go completely mad. As the *Tigris* swung up and down on the swell, the lighthouses flung out what appeared to be long arms where their bases joined and drew them in again just as though they were doing physical jerks to music.

With a calm sea like glass and considerable refraction, he achieved his triumph of sinking a third U-boat. The refraction deceived Lieutenant Coe into thinking that the U-boat was a surface vessel. Anyway, when Lieutenant Coe, D.S.C., on periscope duty, sighted a group of ships, he thought two trawlers were escorting another ship. For three minutes Commander Bone observed the ships before he identified the conning-tower and wireless masts of a U-boat, moving at a brisk pace. The *Tigris* went after her at full speed, gradually coming up until the U-boat was about 3,000 yards away.

The captain ordered the torpedoes to be fired. Within three minutes there were two explosions. Loud bubbling noises and queer banging sounds beat on the ear-drums of the hydrophone operator. They were the death throes of the U-boat. When Commander Bone whipped up his periscope a minute after the explosions, the enemy had disappeared and the trails of the remaining torpedoes were running on into the distance. These gurglings, made by the air escaping from the riven U-boat, continued for twenty minutes. Then all grew still.

His savage blows against the German convoys in northern seas did much to disorganize the enemy's supply lines to Russia and added another six ships to his total besides those which he damaged. On his first patrol, he sank one ship, on his second he sank two, and on his third three.

"There used to be a cathedral calm in the control room when we began an attack," remarked Lieutenant R. P. Reed, who worked the magic machine officially termed the Submarine Torpedo Director, which is so well-known throughout the service as the "fruit machine" that the majority of officers have forgotten its right name. As Commander Bone made his observations concerning the target, Lieutenant Reed turned the various little handles to record the facts from which the machine automatically worked out the angle at which the torpedo should be fired in order to hit the target. It is worth noting that the first model of this miracle-machine was made out of a boy's Meccano set in 1935.

During the day the periscope of the *Tigris* was raised every three minutes for the officer on watch to take a quick look round through the low power periscope for aircraft, before using the high power periscope to make a careful search of each sector of the seas.

While patrolling in these northern latitudes, Commander Bone wore long woollen pants, thick socks, three sweaters, fur-lined flying boots and helmet and an oil-skin suit over all. Asked if he shaved while on patrol, he explained that he shaved every three or four days. "I once grew a beard," he said and my wife hated it when she saw me, so I promised to shave it off the next time I sank a ship. I had to shave four days later," he added.

It was during bad weather that he sighted an enemy convoy steaming up a fiord. He fired a salvo, but a squall blotted out the ships and although he heard two explosions, he could see nothing and therefore made no claim.

"Why doesn't he claim those two ships?" asked members of the crew of each other. "We know he hit them. Why doesn't he claim them?"

They were so enthusiastic that they began to wager among themselves that the *Tigris* had sunk the ships. But Commander Bone, who had no proof, remained silent.

A week later a Russian submarine that was patrolling to the north of the *Tigris* returned to port, and reported that an hour after the *Tigris* had attacked the convoy she sighted it and there were two ships missing. So the luck of Commander Bone stood by him once more.

"Without the crew I could have done nothing," he once remarked. "It was my good fortune to lead some of the keenest and finest men who ever lived." Their keenness welded them into a superb team, each man of whom could be relied upon to perform his special duties directly the Klaxon sounded, and their outstanding work was recognized by the award of the Distinguished Service Medal to fifteen members of the crew, while Lieutenants Bennington, Coe, Hemingway, Jupp and Foster all won the Distinguished Service Cross.

In later days Lieutenant Bennington succeeded to the command of the *Porpoise* and stirred up the enemy in the Mediterranean to an unwonted degree, as was to be expected from an officer who behaved so coolly when the bow of the *Triumph* was blown off by a mine, as described in chapter six. He made British submarine history by carrying petrol in the *Porpoise* to keep the hard-pressed British fighters in the air over Malta during those anxious days when aviation spirit was getting so short that Malta was in danger of succumbing to the continuous attacks of the Luftwaffe. Until the great convoy fought its way through to relieve the island, he rendered invaluable aid, and his secret voyages to and fro became known as the *Porpoise* Carrier Service.

But he packed more than petrol into the *Porpoise*, for on his deck he stacked the deadly mines with which he sowed several cunning minefields, while below with the petrol were stowed the deadlier torpedoes with which he sent one big tanker blazing to the bottom as well as two supply ships. If an enemy bomb or depth charge had caught the *Porpoise* when she was laden like that, it would have touched her off and blasted her out of the sea, but luckily none did.

Certainly it was not for want of trying that the enemy failed to sink the *Porpoise*, for one night Lieutenant Bennington just managed to crash dive to forty feet as a destroyer started to hunt them—a hunt which continued on and off for four nerve-racking days during which the enemy hurled 87 depth charges in his relentless attempt to kill the *Porpoise*. So close were the first three that the shock upset the depth gauge and listening gear and bounced her up in the sea as though she were a switchback. "The whole ship lurched like a lorry going over a big bump in the road," said Sub-Lieutenant C. T. M. Thurlow afterwards. While the depth charges were raining down, Leading-Telegraphist Backman, who won the D.S.M. for his gallantry, calmly located the faults and repaired the listening gear, with the result that he was able to report the movements of the destroyer and enable the *Porpoise* to evade the attacker. Altogether during that patrol the enemy flung 114 depth charges at the *Porpoise*, yet Lieutenant Bennington brought her safely to harbour with her crew unharmed.

Although the Germans built the submarine *Deutschland* to carry cargo across the Atlantic during the last war, it was not until the *Porpoise* returned from the Mediterranean to England at the end of January, 1943, that the Admiralty allowed Lieutenant L. W. A. Bennington, D.S.O., D.S.C., to reveal that in a crisis the submarines of the Royal Navy may adopt the role of tankers and freighters.

To resume the adventures of the *Tigris*, one day she was patrolling in half a gale with squalls of rain and snow occasionally blotting out everything, while the seas added to the difficulties by continually breaking over the periscope to blind the observer. The weather was in fact so bad that the captain was obliged to patrol under the lee of the land in order to gain some protection.

About midday the hydrophone operator reported sounds of a convoy, and Commander Bone steered the *Tigris* to a better attacking position. An hour later he caught a glimpse of a ship of 3,000 tons. She was almost on the spot. There was no time to take her range; if he had attempted it he would have lost her. Having anticipated that something like this might happen some day, he had worked out a plan to meet the eventuality. Immediately he put his plan into operation and fired his torpedoes. A little later, peering through the periscope, Commander Bone saw a big column of black smoke rising from the ship, which gave off dense clouds of smoke for twenty minutes.

The queer thing was that a navigational error led him to fire toward the wrong point of land. If he had fired at the other point of land, as he had planned, he would have missed the ship. What happened was that she changed course while the torpedoes were running, and steamed right into one, much to the delight of the captain and crew of the *Tigris*. It rather looked as though she was determined to commit suicide.

Commander H. F. Bone did magnificent work while commanding His Majesty's submarine *Tigris*. Blessed with keen eyes, a quick brain and those high technical qualifications without which no submarine captain can hope to achieve success, he is convinced that luck also is essential.

He certainly regards himself as lucky, and the way this ship changed course and steamed into his torpedo goes to confirm it. He himself, after describing what happened, summed up the attack quite objectively in these words: "If the ship was destroyed, which all the circumstances indicate, this seems a reasonable solution and is not very abnormal for my personal standard of luck."

The Russians themselves were so appreciative of his courage and skill that they managed to convey to his boat during his last patrol a young reindeer as a tribute from the Russian Commander-in-Chief. It was about the size of a Newfoundland dog, with tiny little bumps where its horns were due to sprout. The crew named it Minsk and once a day the coxswain used to exercise it in the boat before tying it up again in the seamen's washing place. Every two hours when the watch was changed Minsk would get up and bellow and nibble at the seamen's trousers as they passed. After a few days she began to take notice when her name was called. Fed on bread and milk and hay, she made the passage home quite safely, but unfortunately she did not survive.

Not less valuable than his services in sinking enemy ships in those northern waters were the services which Commander Bone rendered in strengthening the bonds of friendship between Russia and Great Britain. The Russians found his actions were much more convincing than words.

May his personal standard of luck continue.

11

FOUR RESCUES

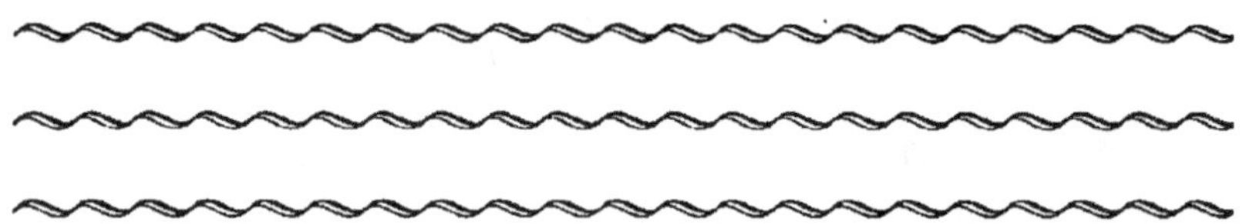

THE people of the British Commonwealth and their Allies will recall with pride that the captains and crews of the submarines of the Royal Navy retained their human sympathy despite the risks inseparable from their calling and in face of the calculated brutality of the Nazis.

It was on Monday, March 18, 1940, that the Dutch trawler *Protinus* pulled out of the port of Ymuiden to fish near the Middle Rough Bank, in days when Holland was still hypnotized into thinking that the word neutrality created a sanctuary from the sufferings of war—although Hitler had already committed the Rotterdam atrocity on paper to prepare for the awful reality that followed.

To ensure that the Germans would not mistake her for an enemy, the *Protinus* had been marked in seven places with Dutch markings and the crew fished without fear, under the impression that their flag would protect them from outrage. At 6.30 on the evening of March 20th, when they were twenty miles north-west of the Middle Rough Bank, a large monoplane marked with white crosses and swastikas suddenly dived out of the skies. The crew heard the deadly rattle of its machine-guns as it swooped over. They watched it turn to come back. This time it dropped seven bombs, one of which hit the bridge. By the time it came over the third time, the crew were waving their Dutch flag, but the Germans greeted this sign of neutrality by dropping five more bombs, which all missed. A fourth attack was made with five bombs, one of which wrecked the engine-room, and killed the captain and a seaman, a fireman and trimmer being wounded.

With the trawler sinking under them, the eight survivors, including the two wounded, took to the boat and saw the *Protinus* sink twenty minutes later. They had no food and no compass, and only a little brackish water to sustain them in their attempt to reach the Danish coast. After dark the aircraft was heard to come back three times as if in search of them, but fortunately the night cheated the murderers of further victims.

The cold winds and seas bit into the Dutchmen as they huddled in the boat. The wounded men grew weaker until on the morning of March 25th they slept for good and were buried at sea.

That evening, just about 6 o'clock, Lieutenant J. N. A. Low, who was on the bridge of the *Unity*, sighted the small boat just over half a mile away. The captain of the *Unity*, Lieutenant-Commander J. F. B. Brown, came to the bridge and examined the boat through his glasses.

"Show them the ensign," he ordered. As the white ensign was hung over the bridge there was a faint cheer from the boat and one or two men waved. Making a careful search of the seas to make sure that the boat was not being used as a decoy by a U-boat, the captain brought the *Unity* alongside and rescued the survivors.

It was not easy. All suffered badly from exposure. Three were so weak that members of the *Unity's* crew had to get down on the fore hydroplanes and haul them on board with bowlines. Life was at such a low ebb that these poor fellows imagined they were being taken prisoner by a U-boat and they were not interested in their rescue until the sight of the white ensign gradually impressed upon their suffering minds that they were on a British ship. Then their dull eyes kindled and their whole attitude changed.

No men could have been kinder than the crew of the *Unity*, who stripped the soddened clothes from the survivors, rubbed them down and tended to their every want. Let me record the words of Lieutenant-Commander Brown: "I wish to pay a tribute to the extremely fine and unselfish spirit displayed by the sailors whom I have the honour to command in their dealings with the survivors of the *Protinus*. Not only did they cheerfully sacrifice their very limited sleeping accommodation to these men, but all ratings gave up a very considerable amount of their time, time which especially during the foul weather experienced on the trip to base, was extremely precious to them, massaging the extremities of the survivors, fetching them water and generally administering to them. The fine example set by Lieutenant Low and Petty Officer R. Knott was undoubtedly largely responsible for this."

The Dutch fishermen suffered so badly from exposure that three days after they were rescued only one man had regained any feeling in his feet. Three of them were in such pain as the blood strove to circulate in their limbs that it was necessary to give them morphia. In two cases when the men reached a Scottish hospital amputations were necessary to save their lives and they were still in hospital two years after their rescue.

For their humane act in rescuing and caring for the Dutchmen the captain, officers and crew of the *Unity* were thanked officially by the Chief of the Netherlands Naval Staff who expressed the gratitude and appreciation of the Dutch nation.

Some months later, on July 29, 1940, Lieutenant P. J. Cowell was patrolling off the Norwegian coast in the *Swordfish* when he rescued four officers of the Norwegian Merchant Service who were trying to escape to England in the little yacht *Maski* which had lost her sails and rudder in the rough seas and was drifting helplessly. The Norwegians were delighted to be picked up, and in the words of the captain of the *Swordfish*, who paid them the rare honour of taking them with him on patrol, during which time they acted as look-outs and performed other duties: "Their behaviour in such unusual surroundings was magnificent."

They proved to be a certificated master mariner, two first mates and an engineer and were so impressed with their experience of a British submarine on active service and the high morale and efficiency of the crew that they expressed the greatest enthusiasm to the Norwegian Admiralty.

There is no space to mention all the rescues effected by British submarines, but the case of the *Tropic Sea* was rather unusual. It was on August 30, 1940, that Lieutenant-Commander H. A. V. Haggard left a Scottish base to take the *Truant* out to the Mediterranean, where he sank several ships including a 9,000 ton tanker—incidentally when his torpedo hit this tanker early on December 16, 1940, there was such a small flash that he mistook it for the flash of the tanker's gun firing back at him and promptly fired two more torpedoes at short range—whereupon the tanker disappeared in a few seconds.

He was less lucky with another tanker which his careful reconnaissance of a North African harbour revealed beside the quay. A series of shoals protected the harbour from submarines, quite apart from other defences, but to Lieutenant-Commander Haggard these were of no moment compared with the necessity of destroying the tanker. Accordingly he felt his way through the shoals until he reached the buoy marking the harbour entrance. Here he lurked until it was nearly dark, then he crept right inside the harbour. His courage and boldness deserved success.

By now it was quite dark, but he managed to locate the tanker in silhouette against the traffic lights ashore and fired two torpedoes at her. He was only 400 yards away, and it seemed impossible that he could miss. Nevertheless, both his torpedoes passed beneath her—one exploded ashore in a shower of golden rain, while the other went up in a cloud of dense smoke.

Before he could turn and run for it, it was essential to bring the *Truant* right up to the surface. As he swung round and slipped past the tanker, an Italian leaned over the rail, jabbering for all he was worth; he seemed a trifle upset as he shouted after the vanishing submarine: "Il Duce!"

To revert to the *Tropic Sea*, the *Truant* by September 3, 1940, was well across the Bay of Biscay when the look-out sighted masts and funnels peeping over the horizon to the east just before 7 o'clock in the morning. Lieutenant-Commander Haggard, judging that the steamer was making for Bordeaux, went toward her at speed and on drawing nigh saw that she was heavily laden and bore some resemblance to a Norwegian ship, although he could not identify her.

"Order her not to transmit any wireless messages

and to stop her engines and send across the captain with his papers," said Lieutenant-Commander Haggard to his signalman who flashed the orders in international code.

The steamer duly came to a standstill, while the *Truant* stopped half a mile away with her guns ready to open fire. There was considerable activity aboard, with an abnormal number of men for a cargo steamer. After a time it seemed obvious that they were going to abandon ship. Eventually all the boats were lowered and pulled clear, but the *Truant's* signals to send the captain were completely ignored. At last the *Truant* went over to find him, and he was discovered and taken on board the *Truant* for questioning, just as two explosions occurred and two large holes were blown in the side of the steamer.

She was the Norwegian steamer *Tropic Sea*, captured by a German raider near Norfolk Island on April 24, 1940. The raider already had on board the crew of the British steamer *Haxby* which had been sunk by gunfire on April 6th. Transferring the British prisoners to the *Tropic Sea*, the captain put on board a German prize crew with instructions to work the steamer and her valuable cargo of 8,000 tons of wheat to France.

That was no light undertaking. Norfolk Island is some 1,100 miles to the north of Auckland, New Zealand, and whether the German captain took the *Tropic Sea* eastward, dodging from island to island across the Pacific and round Cape Horn to steal northward up the Southern Atlantic to France, or whether he steamed westward across the Indian Ocean and round the Cape of Good Hope to his destination, he had to reckon on a voyage of roughly 12,000 miles or so before reaching port.

The Germans, as in the case of the *Altmark*, used the *Tropic Sea* as a prison ship, hoping to convey their British prisoners to the hardships of a concentration camp. For thousands of miles she crept across the ocean. For months her propellers turned and brought the British prisoners ever nearer to captivity. The German captain must have been congratulating himself on having accomplished a supremely difficult feat when the *Truant* suddenly appeared and completely turned the tables, nullifying months of toil and scheming.

The German captain carried out the usual Nazi procedure of scuttling his ship, placing six bombs for that purpose. Four of them were still unexploded as Lieutenant-Commander Haggard questioned him, before replacing him in the lifeboat with the injunction that he was responsible for the lives of every man in the boats. The twenty-three members of the crew of the *Haxby*, who were so unexpectedly snatched from captivity, were taken on board the *Truant* along with the Norwegian captain of the *Tropic Sea* and his wife. It was impossible for the *Truant* to rescue more without jeopardizing her own safety.

As the *Tropic Sea* continued to float, the Norwegian captain offered to try to work her to port with his own crew who were in the boats with the Germans. But she took a list and sank while he was discussing the chances with the *Truant's* captain.

Resuming his voyage to Gibraltar, Lieutenant-Commander Haggard signalled to base, and next day at dawn a Sunderland flying-boat was sent out from Calshot on its errand of mercy to pick up the men who were left in the boats. Both lifeboats were equipped with sails and the sea was a flat calm, so the men in the boats were in no immediate danger. The Sunderland eventually located them and rescued the ten Norwegian seamen from the fate to which the Germans had condemned them. Their added weight made it difficult for the captain of the Sunderland to take off again, but he managed it and brought them back to England safely.

The following day the Sunderland flew out to pick up the Germans, and take them prisoner, but by the time the flying-boat arrived in the area there was a spanking breeze blowing directly towards the coast and no trace of the boats to be seen, so it is probable that the enemy escaped to Spain.

It was the rare case of a submarine and a flying-boat co-operating to rescue British and Norwegian captives.

The *Thetis* will always be associated with the tragedy of Liverpool Bay on June 1, 1939, and custom decreed that her name should be banished from the roll of the Royal Navy. In her place a *Thunderbolt* rose from the depths to smite the enemy and she had no sooner put to sea under the command of Lieutenant-Commander C. B. Crouch than she began to justify her title. Any unhappy memories that may have clung to her from a former incarnation were dispelled during her first patrol in December, 1940, when her captain achieved the distinction of sinking a U-boat. The *Thunderbolt* resembled a cricketer who went in on a sticky wicket and scored off the first ball. It was a good augury.

That patrol, which started on December 3, 1940, began to get interesting about 8:30 on the morning of December 15th when the captain detected something off the French coast which looked like the conning-tower of a submarine. A little later, however, he made out two trawlers, and as smoke appeared to come from the other vessel, he concluded they were three trawlers he had seen previously and changed the course of the *Thunderbolt* to regain his patrol position. Yet some uncertainty still remained, and he was carefully studying the group of ships about 9 o'clock when he detected a U-boat among the three trawlers which were then three miles away. There was a fairly heavy swell, with a strong wind and a bright sun as he moved in to reduce the range by half a mile before firing a torpedo at the U-boat.

Through his periscope he saw a column of water mounting into the sky, after a brief interval he observed one end of the U-boat sticking up out of the water, and when he looked again it had vanished.

The *Thunderbolt* had hurled her first bolt to destroy the enemy.

This initial patrol was the prelude to others in the Mediterranean during which the successes of Lieutenant-Commander Crouch gradually mounted until they totalled two U-boats and five supply ships and won for him the D.S.O. and Bar. But of all his successes, probably that which gave him the greatest pleasure was the rescue of forty-three men and a dog who were the survivors of a merchantman sunk in the Mediterranean in July, 1941. Somehow he managed to embark them all on board the *Thunderbolt*. They brought his complement up to 111 and as there is never any space to spare on a submarine it can be imagined that the boat was rather crowded. But somehow the captain packed them all in and was able to feed them and find corners for them to sleep in for three days while he made his way back to port. It was a rescue which was admirably summed up as "a fine effort."

12

A MESSAGE IN CODE

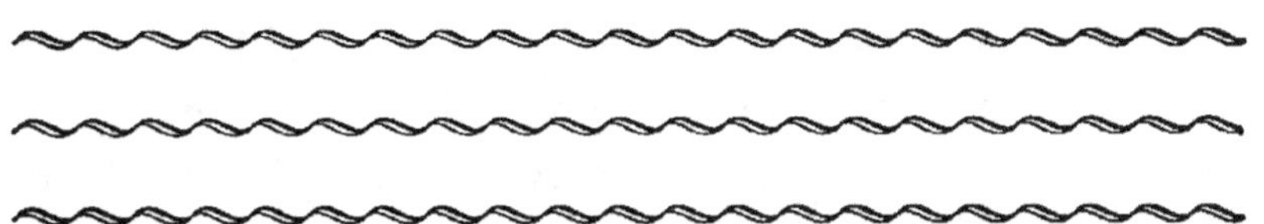

KNOWN throughout the submarine services as Jacky, which indicates his popularity, Commander Jack Etheridge Slaughter won his spurs and the D.S.O. by a triple triumph against the German ships during the invasion of Norway in April, 1940. He was born on May 21, 1905, at Reading—the city of biscuits, beer and seeds, as he once tersely described it—and evidently the spirit of his grandfather, who was a captain in the Royal Navy, inspired him, for throughout his early years he was bent on going to sea. As the Nautical College, Pangbourne, set amid the sylvan reaches of the Thames, was close to Reading, he began his studies there before passing through Dartmouth to become a midshipman in the Royal Navy. To-day he stands 5 feet 11 inches tall, and both in face and form Charles Laughton bears a remarkable resemblance to him, although it is problematical whether the actor possesses a more profound knowledge of English than the sailor.

Assuming command of the *Sunfish* when she passed out of dockyard hands, Commander Slaughter, after a few uneventful patrols went off to patrol in Heligoland Bight. A whisper that the big ships of the German fleet were out failed to give any indication of their whereabouts, but Commander Slaughter asked for nothing more than a sight of them through his periscope. The weather for weeks had been very severe. Great stretches of sea off Scandinavia were frozen, in some cases as far as thirty miles from the shore, and it was thought that the sea around Heligoland was also frozen but Commander Slaughter learned otherwise.

A few weeks later he was on patrol off the northern coast of Denmark. Hitler had subjugated Poland, the Germans had driven the French forces which had irrupted into the Ruhr back to the Maginot Line. The international situation was tense. Scandinavia, Denmark, Holland and Belgium were hushed as in a trance, waiting and wondering what Hitler would do.

At 6 o'clock in the evening the *Sunfish* was patrolling in the Skagerrak off the Skaw when Commander Slaughter beheld the one thing he wished to see. In the little lens of the periscope loomed three German cruisers, protected by a screen of four or five destroyers. Studying the cruisers, he made them out to be the *Hipper*, the *Blucher* and another which he could not identify. He was in a good position to attack and the high-pitched buzz of the alarm instantly brought the crew to their stations. With taut nerves he manipulated the periscope and turned the knob of the range-finder at the side. Here was the chance of a lifetime. Just as he started to give his orders to prepare for the attack his hopes were smashed. He watched with fascinated eye while his face grew red with pent-up emotion. Almost at the moment of sighting them, the German ships turned away.

"Unfortunately they made a big alteration of course—it was sixty degrees—and that left me right out in the deep field," he said, when the keen edge had worn off his disappointment. "I had feelings of utter despair and I was tempted to fire a salvo of torpedoes—but I never for one moment regretted not doing it."

If words could have blasted the German fleet off the seas, the enemy would have been instantly vanquished.

"What did you say?" he was once said.

"My remarks were unprintable," he answered truthfully with a smile.

Next day he was called by the officer of the watch. "Some trawlers are approaching, sir."

The *Sunfish* was diving, so he altered course towards them, meaning no harm, thinking they were just fishing trawlers. He was slightly more than a mile away when the trawlers suddenly changed course straight for him, and he realized that they were anti-submarine trawlers out to kill him if they could.

"We had a very interesting two hours after that,"

was his comment on the hunt which followed. He was too clever for them and managed to shake them off.

Next day Commander Slaughter sighted a German transport of 4,000 tons. It was steaming north heavily laden, with the Nazi flag trailing in the wind. At that moment the International Regulations governing submarine warfare were still crippling the efforts of British submarine officers who were ordered strictly to obey the regulations, although the Germans paid no attention to them whatsoever. Before Commander Slaughter could do anything to the transport he was bound by the regulations to stop her and ensure the safety of all on board. It was an impossible situation, with the Germans ignoring the rules and Great Britain still madly observing them.

Commander Slaughter was tied. He could do nothing to the German transport except let it pass on its way flaunting its vile flag. "Anyway, if I can't use her as a real target, I'll use her as a dummy one and practice a diving attack on her," he thought.

Altering course, he began to work into position to make his dummy attack. As he did so a message came to him from the engineer officer who acted as coding officer. "Among a batch of signals being decoded there is one which may have some bearing on this attack, sir."

"All right. Relay the message to me as it is decoded word by word," ordered Commander Slaughter, who gave instructions for torpedoes to be got ready as he continued to steer the *Sunfish* into position for his dummy attack.

It was about 3 o'clock in the afternoon. The day was sunny, the sea calm, and the transport was quite close to the shore. Word by word the Admiralty message was relayed to Commander Slaughter as he gazed into the periscope. Just as the Nazi transport started to come into his sights he grew suddenly tense. He listened eagerly. Word by word the message was decoded. Closer and closer the transport approached to the firing position. Commander Slaughter stood there in the control room, wondering what the Admiralty was going to say. The suspense was almost unbearable. She was exactly on the spot when the message gave him permission to attack.

"Fire" ordered Commander Slaughter.

It was an astonishing coincidence. He received those last words of the Admiralty message amending his previous instructions at the same instant that the ship came right in his sights.

He watched the white wake of the torpedoes rushing toward the transport, saw one torpedo hit and explode amidships. She had no escort. For the moment he had nothing to fear. The sun shone brightly as the Germans took to the boats to pull ashore.

If Commander Slaughter was inclined to rail at Fate for playing him a scurvy trick over the German fleet, he had cause to thank his incredible luck in receiving the Admiralty message just in time to sink the transport. Whether it was just luck, or prevision which induced him to carry out that dummy attack which ended in a triumph, who shall say?

"I thought I'd nip in under her tail to see who she was, but I sighted some trawlers and said to myself— 'This is no place for us. We'll get away from the body.'" Which he did.

For five days the *Sunfish* was harried ceaselessly in the Skagerrak while the German invasion of Norway went on. But he made the Germans pay. The crew were tired out by their ceaseless vigils. The battery was low, and Commander Slaughter, wanting a place where he could rest, sat quietly on the bottom.

At the requisite time he came up to periscope depth. Within five minutes he saw a transport of 6,000 tons approaching while an escort of trawlers were grouped astern to guard her.

Making a quick attack, he watched one of his torpedoes hit amidships. Then he saw the Germans scurry into the boats, while the transport carried on and piled up on the rocks where she took a big list. Soon the hunters got busy, so he calmly went to ground.

That night he was due to finish his patrol. Just about dusk, when it was becoming rather difficult to see through the periscope, he sighted a 5,000 ton ship which looked as though it might pass within range. The escorting trawlers were zigzagging about all over the place, obviously very frightened by the news that a ship had already been torpedoed there a few hours earlier.

He had three torpedoes left. "I shall want one on the way home," he thought. "I'll have a crack and give her two." He could just see her through the high-power periscope, and it seemed rather a forlorn hope.

"I took a chance and fired and to my complete astonishment I got two hits," he said in the wardroom on his return.

The passage back was not without its excitements. One engine of the *Sunfish* was out of commission owing to a faulty piston, so Commander Slaughter decided to replace it going through the Skagerrak. After sweating over it about twelve hours to get it out, the air inside the *Sunfish* grew rather fuggy, so the captain determined to surface for a refresher. A couple of minutes later the look-out shouted: "Look!"

"He pointed to three of the largest aircraft I have ever seen in my life. I thought, 'this is the end,'" the captain said. "We were such a long time getting down that I thought we couldn't possibly escape—but we did: they must have been troop carriers."

The great aircraft passed without attacking, and about 2 o'clock in the morning the engineer got the new piston into place. It had been a long struggle and a hard one, lasting about twenty-six hours. The difficulties of changing a piston in the circumscribed space of a submarine while she is at sea are immense.

They were congratulating themselves on a job well done when the engineer discovered that it was impossible to connect up.

Think of their feelings after all their toil. Someone

called it a ghastly discovery, but what the captain called it is known to the engine-room staff alone.

There was only one thing to be done, so they set about replacing the faulty piston. But if the man who made that blunder could have been in the *Sunfish* at that moment, he would have vowed never again to do anything without properly checking it. That careless oversight might have led to the destruction of a submarine and her entire crew.

In due course the *Sunfish* glided on her motors across the waters at her base. Forward and aft stood members of the crew with heaving lines in their hands. The propellers of the *Sunfish* were reversed, churning up the peaceful waters in a flurry of foam to take the way off her. She slid gently alongside the depot ship. Tiny spots of oil bobbed up here and there to form rainbow discs of colour on the surface. The heaving lines shot out toward the waiting men on the depot ship who quickly hauled in the hawsers and made her fast.

The *Sunfish* was safely home again.

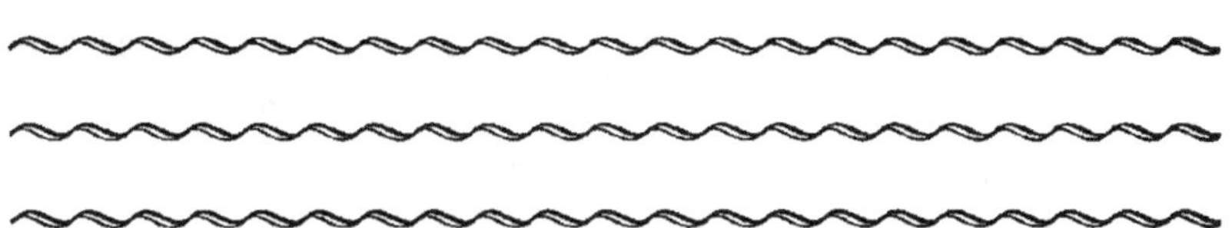

DISABLED

To DESCRIBE the career of a submarine as a series of ups and downs would be figuratively as well as literally true, for every time she rises to periscope depth to inflict trouble on the enemy she usually dives away to escape the trouble threatening herself. The *Taku* was no exception, as was proved during her patrol off the Norwegian coast in the first half of May, 1940.

Lieutenant-Commander V. J. Van der Byl arrived in his allotted area to find the sea like a sheet of glass, clear as the Mediterranean, and decidedly unfavourable for harrying the Germans off the Norwegian coast. Nevertheless he started in search of any quarry that came within range. But nothing was seen for some days, throughout which he was unable to fix his position by sun or star, and not until 2:30 p.m. on May 8th was he able to use his sextant to take a sight of the sun through the clouds.

An hour later a Dornier flying boat appeared. Now

a submarine officer knows that an aircraft may be the advance guard of a surface ship, and all he can do is to wait hopefully and use his periscope when opportunity serves.

This is what the captain of the *Taku* did. A bomb exploding close by warned him that the enemy was on the watch, and a second bomb, even closer, made him steer the *Taku* deeper to avoid the danger. The celerity with which the *Taku* was attacked on raising her periscope strengthened his assumption that ships were not far away—an assumption that was soon confirmed by the hydrophone operator who caught the sounds of their engines.

Steering up to periscope depth, the captain glanced through the periscope. There were two fine merchant ships each of 8,000 tons, cleverly camouflaged and escorted by two torpedo boats while two large aircraft patrolled overhead. Only valuable steamers would have been provided with so strong an escort. The torpedo boats were zigzagging about to protect the ships while the aircraft were circling in the sky to search the seas around.

It took the captain of the *Taku* twenty minutes to work into position to fire his torpedoes, during which time he observed the speed and course of the merchantmen.

"Fire!" he ordered.

The captain took the *Taku* down and away at full speed to dodge the forthcoming attack. One minute after the last torpedo was fired, there were three explosions to prove that three of his torpedoes had struck home.

At once the enemy let loose his fury and, as the captain noted, "A perfect avalanche of depth charges rained down."

To meet the attack, he cut the speed of the *Taku* in order to lessen the sound of the motors and make it more difficult for the hunters to track him. The trim of the submarine was already upset by firing the torpedoes. As soon as her speed was reduced she dived for fifty feet, cannoned against the bottom and bounced up again for thirty feet. While she was cutting these dangerous capers the first lieutenant struggled to adjust the trim and get her under control, but it was impossible to hold her and she dropped back again to the seabed.

To avoid further risk, Lieutenant-Commander Van der Byl promptly stopped the motors and let her rest. The hydrophone operator heard the hunters rushing about on the surface trying to locate the *Taku*, whose captain set his wits to work to defeat them. The gyroscope droned away. "Cover it with a blanket," he ordered and verily blanketed the sound. Very cleverly he adjusted the trim to prevent the depth charges from forcing him to the surface. A stillness settled in the boat. Above it the sound of leaking water assumed the dimensions of a devastating noise that threatened to give away their position and lead to their destruction. It turned out to be a leak from one of the torpedo tubes into the control room bilge. Then someone with a genius for improvisation had the idea of using a funnel and a length of rubber pipe to conduct the water silently away to a bathroom. After that the sounds ceased.

The hydrophone operator heard the torpedo boats start systematically to hunt.

Just after 6 o'clock in the evening the attack became intense. Every two minutes a depth charge came down and exploded. The *Taku* rocked and shook. A gauge glass was smashed. The forward hatch was lifted by one explosion and began to leak slightly. But the clamps held and averted serious danger. It was a nervy business, waiting for the next charge to explode, wondering if the luck of the *Taku* would still hold.

Yet the men remained calm. They were more than calm, they were actually cheerful. Leading Stoker W. G. Pearson had endured the gruelling time in the *Spearfish*, and somebody asked him: "How does this compare with the *Spearfish*?"

"Not so bad! Not nearly so!" he replied cheerfully.

Nevertheless they were relieved when that attack eased off after twenty-four minutes. They rested, talking in whispers, waiting for it to start again. Some dozed, several read, as though they were waiting in a train that was held up in a tunnel.

One of the most amazing scenes of all was the sight of two men playing draughts. The third officer and the engineer officer in that moment of ordeal, with the danger of instant death hanging over them, were so much the masters of their souls that they could bring an air of detachment to bear which enabled them to enjoy a game of draughts. They were quite absorbed as they pushed the men forward, each seeking to trap the other and vanquish him, just as the Germans were seeking to trap and destroy them.

The enemy hunted the *Taku* doggedly up to 10:30 that night. Then the sounds of the hunters faded.

Allowing another hour to pass, in order to be on the safe side, the captain of the *Taku* decided to surface. Taking every precaution to eliminate as much noise as possible, passing all orders by word of mouth instead of telephone, he gradually blew the main ballast tanks. But it was twenty minutes before the *Taku* came unstuck from the bottom and lifted in her bed. As he moved forward on one motor to get as far away from the area as possible before coming to the surface, he had a misgiving, for the sound of a ship was heard passing slowly up one side and ahead of the submarine. For a moment Lieutenant-Commander Van der Byl thought he had been detected. But the sound died away and an hour later he steered the *Taku* to the surface to let the high pressure air out of the boat and allow the crew to fill their lungs with the sweet air as they recharged the batteries for the dawn patrol. Miles away in the darkness the lights of some fishing vessels twinkled. Of the enemy there was no sign.

If the *Taku* suffered a little more after an attack she made on November 2, 1940, she had only herself to blame and brought it on by hitting the enemy so hard that the blow rebounded upon her. She was then commanded by Lieutenant-Commander J. F. B. Brown, D.S.C., who had previously commanded the *Unity*.

She was on the surface off the French coast in the early morning of November 2nd, with Lieutenant H. B. Turner serving as officer of the watch on the bridge and Petty Officer A. Martin as the foremost look-out. It was quite clear, but so dark and moonless that it was not possible to see much beyond a mile. As it happened, Lieutenant Turner had made a special study of night observations and had therefore paid particular attention to training the look-outs of the *Taku*. During the hours of darkness when a submarine is on the surface, the lives of all on board depend upon the alertness of the look-outs. The men who can see quickest and furthest are the men on whom success in attack or defense depends.

"Object on the starboard bow, sir," said Petty Officer Martin.

Lieutenant Turner ranged with his glasses and made out the object to be a large tanker about a mile away on the edge of visibility. Altering the helm of the submarine to gain an attacking position, he called the captain, who scanned the tanker and gave instructions about setting the torpedoes, while Lieutenant Turner manipulated the night sights.

Eight minutes after locating the tanker, Lieutenant-Commander Brown gave the order to fire. A salvo of torpedoes sped toward the target. The tanker was but half a mile away. Within 30 seconds there was a heavy explosion, followed five seconds later by a second and a third.

The blast of the explosion hit the *Taku* before she could dive and not only cracked some of her castings, but smashed some depth gauges and did other damage. The queer thing was that in the brief period before diving, Lieutenant-Commander Brown could detect no sign of damage to the tanker.

Yet she was mortally wounded, for no sound came from her engines after the explosion, and when the captain of the *Taku* came to the surface ten minutes later, there was no trace of the tanker, but the wind was charged with the fumes of fuel oil.

The tanker was steaming without an escort, no doubt hoping that the intense darkness of the night would cover her movements until she made port, but the keen eyes of the look-out of the *Taku* penetrated the darkness and enabled the well-aimed torpedoes of the captain to send her to the bottom. It was a triumph for Lieutenant-Commander Brown as well as a tribute to the training and skill of Lieutenant Turner.

Yet all the fights Lieutenant-Commander Brown had with the enemy were probably overshadowed by one he had with the sea in 1941. Cruising into the Atlantic, he noted the second day out that the barometer was falling sharply. The sea was calm, with a light wind, but the barometer indicated that bad weather was brewing.

The following day was ushered in with a fresh wind, which by 4 o'clock in the morning had increased to 16 miles an hour. Two hours later it had doubled in force and grown to half a gale with a very high sea.

The *Taku* staggered and rolled under the impact of the seas. The huge waves washed over the bridge time and again and flooded the control room, until it became so bad that the captain was forced to heave-to at 6:30 in the morning, when he was about 750 miles out in the Atlantic: Keeping her head to wind under the power of the engines, he decided to ride out the gale.

It grew in fury. The wind howled through the jumping wires. The seas bore down on her and crashed against the bridge with immense force. She swung up on the crests and pitched down the other side. By breakfast time the wind was touching nearly sixty miles an hour and the seas were still rising. A little later the bow of the *Taku* began to fall away. No longer pushing her nose into the wind, she gradually veered until she almost wallowed in the troughs, beam on to the seas.

She began to roll so dangerously that Lieutenant-Commander Brown ordered the engines to be stopped, at once closed the conning-tower hatch and switched on the motors in order to bring her head to wind again. In one respect he was better off than a surface ship: by shutting the conning-tower hatch he could keep the seas out, whereas a surface ship caught in a similar position might start rolling until she rolled right over and went to the bottom.

Slowly under the power of the motors he brought her head into the wind again. It was no easy task, and took about a quarter of an hour. He could not understand why she had fallen off at all. Each time she swung up on a crest, she pitched to leeward as she slid down into the trough. Puzzling over her strange behaviour, he concluded that as she pitched to leeward her helm and the engines were unable to overcome this tendency, with the result that she swung beam on.

Opening up the hatch again, he restarted the main engines. For a short time all went well. Then she began to fall away until she was in the same predicament as before.

Once more the captain closed the hatch, switched on the motors and struggled to work her head into the wind. When at length he succeeded, he opened the hatch and turned over to the main engines. But it was useless. The *Taku* seemed to be possessed of a devil. She swung beam on for the third time, and for the third time he shut the hatch and switched on the motors to bring her back into the wind so that she could ride the seas in safety.

This time he tried in vain. Neither his seamanship nor the power of the motors could overcome her strange tendency which made her jib at the seas and swing round. Some mysterious force was compelling her to do something unnatural. What was it?

Considering the problem, he remembered that the *Triad* had been caught in a gale which jammed her after hydroplanes in a vertical position. Had the same mishap befallen the *Taku*? He wondered.

He had no means of finding out except by seeing, and it was the middle of the afternoon before the *Taku* dipped her nose so deep and swung her stern so high out of the sea that he caught a glimpse of her after hydroplanes from the bridge. They were, as he had suspected, jammed in a vertical position. She was out of hand; it was useless to attempt to control her. Lashing the officer of the watch and the look-out to the periscope standards to prevent them from being washed overboard, he closed the conning-tower hatch again to safeguard his ship and waited to send a signal to base.

The two men, lashed to the periscope standards, facing the fury of the gale and slashed by the wicked seas, kept watch to prevent an enemy stealing on them unawares and surprising their comrades shut up in that steel tube. It is a picture to remember when trifles ashore become irksome.

Just before midnight the captain signalled for assistance. Unable to take a sight, he could not fix his position with certainty, and it was difficult to judge how fast he was drifting and exactly in which direction. The wind was still howling at about sixty miles an hour, the seas were running higher than ever.

By 4 o'clock next morning, however, the wind had eased to forty miles an hour. Throughout the day it dropped until by 10 o'clock that night it had moderated to a twenty-five mile breeze.

For three days the *Taku* lay at the mercy of the sea as well as of her enemies, for the gale had wrought damage which made it impossible to train the gun; but she sighted neither friend nor foe.

Lieutenant-Commander Brown was by no means beaten. The wind was westerly, and to the east over the far horizon was England. The wind blew Nelson to victory, and it might still blow the *Taku* safely home if some plan could be devised for sailing her. "See if you can work out a sail plan," said the captain to Lieutenant H. B. Turner. That officer, setting to work, produced a plan and prepared the necessary gear, and the captain and his officers and men were determined, if assistance failed them, to do their best to sail the helpless submarine back to England.

Luckily help came. The *Taku's* signal brought the famous Admiralty yacht *Enchantress* as well as the *Gladiolus* and the tug *Salvonia* to the rescue, with Lieutenant P. J. Cowell, D.S.C., on board the rescue tug to lend his expert aid. March 3rd was not an hour old when the look-outs on the *Taku* sighted the *Enchantress* whose captain had managed to locate them notwithstanding the distance they had drifted. The two ships exchanged signals, and then the crew of the *Taku* waited patiently for the appearance of the rescue tug and the corvette *Gladiolus*. They arrived about mid-day and a couple of hours later the rescue tug fired a rocket across the submarine's bridge, but unfortunatley the line broke before the towing wire could be hauled over, and conditions were too bad to make another attempt that day.

The length of 5-inch towing wire, which was joined up on the tug to a gigantic 18-inch hawser, was of course so heavy that to manhandle it from the submarine was impracticable. Power was necessary and this the *Taku* had in plenty, although her construction made it useless in the circumstances, for a cable could not be led over her deck, down through the conning-tower and along into the engine room. A straight haul was essential and as the submarine could not pull the cable across, the rescuers seemed to be faced with an insoluble problem. Far from it being insoluble, however, they solved it cleverly in the following simple manner.

Early next morning, when the second attempt was made to pass the tow to the submarine, the captain of the *Taku* started operations by fitting a sail to a raft and floating it over to the tug. A block reeved with a 3-inch manila rope was tied to the raft, which was then hauled back to the submarine while a man on the tug paid out the double lines and retained the two ends on the tug: the rope thus formed a long loop running through the block on the *Taku* back to the tug. To one end of this rope was attached a huge 5-inch block along with the 5-inch towing wire; the other end of the rope was slipped over the tug's capstan which hauled the heavy gear over to the submarine as it wound in the rope through the block on the *Taku*. It was a brilliant way of solving a difficult problem.

The towing wire was soon made fast on the submarine and very gradually the tug took up the strain and got her on the move. This is always an anxious moment in starting to tow, for if the tug took up the slack too quickly, the immense weight of the ship at the other end of the steel cable would snap it as though it were a silken thread. The commanding officer of the tug *Salvonia* was far too experienced to make this mistake. Gradually he forged ahead until he was steaming about two knots, which he maintained all day in heavy weather. About 6 o'clock that evening those on the tug felt an unexpected jerk as one of the shackles on the *Taku* parted, apparently because the towing wire fouled some piece of floating wreckage.

It proved a difficult business to haul in the towing wire. By the time it was safely housed, the light was beginning to fail. With the weather worsening as darkness came on, it became necessary to relinquish operations, consequently the tug cruised around in the vicinity of the submarine all night. Next day the weather was so foul that it was hopeless to approach the disabled *Taku*, for the seas were running too high to attempt to get a line to her and the tug herself was badly buffeted.

Just before 8 o'clock next morning the *Salvonia*

came up with the *Taku*. It was still blowing hard, the seas were very rough, but in spite of these seemingly impossible conditions the rescuers decided to try again. Manœuvring the tug into position, those on board attached a line to a lifebuoy which they floated to leeward of the submarine until she drifted down on it and picked it up. The usual procedure started; and the wire was about half way across when the line parted.

Conditions were too bad and the seas too rough to expect success, but the men who had taken on the job were determined to carry it through. While the towing wire was being wound in, the captain of the *Enchantress* pumped oil to the windward of the *Taku* and as this spread over the surface it calmed the seas sufficiently to enable the towing wire to be hauled on board the submarine.

Exercising consummate skill in the rough seas, the captain of the rescue tug took up the weight of the *Taku* and got her moving again. He clung to her grimly throughout the day despite the gale and heavy swell, while the *Enchantress* and the *Gladiolus* acted as escorts.

All the night the tug crawled over the Atlantic, creeping nearer and nearer to safety. Anxious eyes watched the towing gear for fear it should part again. It was under a heavy strain in those turbulent seas, but it stood up well.

On the following day an aircraft arrived overhead to act as air guard, and the weather moderated sufficiently for the tug to work up to four knots, at which speed the *Salvonia* brought the *Taku* to safety, fifteen days after she was disabled by the gale.

In calm seas the towing of the *Taku* would have been a fine feat; in the prevailing rough weather it was magnificent. No officer could have shown more resource or given better technical advice during these difficult operations than Lieutenant P. J. Cowell, and no captain could have handled his ship more skilfully than the commanding officer of the rescue tug *Salvonia* or toiled harder than the captain, officers and crew of the *Taku*. They merited every word of praise that was bestowed upon them by the Admiralty.

It was during the night of November 26-27, 1939, that Lieutenant-Commander R. Mc. P. Jonas discovered that the *Triad* was not behaving normally and that her engines could not hold her in the teeth of the heavy seas and gale. The engineer found nothing inside the boat to account for it, but the captain soon discovered that she was drifting toward a shoal at about three knots, because the hydroplanes had become fixed in an upright position. The situation was critical, for if she grounded, it seemed impossible for her to avoid being pounded to pieces by the immense seas. Nearer and nearer she drifted. More and more her bow swung round. The captain watched anxiously. She was barely two hundred yards from the seas breaking on the edge of the shoal when she swung round sufficiently to enable the captain to save her from grounding by reversing the engines and going astern to draw clear. It was a narrow escape.

That was the start of the captain's troubles. The *Triad* was disabled almost at the door of the enemy and all he could do was to crawl astern at 2 knots. He signalled for help, and for a couple of hours H.M.S. *Inglefield* managed to tow the *Triad*. Then the tow broke and for a day and a half while vain efforts were made to take her in tow again she continued to go astern until she covered a distance of 74 sea miles. For about four days the Germans had her at their mercy, yet they failed to strike.

Finding it impossible to tow her back to England, H.M.S. *Inglefield* eventually towed her into Stavanger Fiord, where the Norwegian naval authorities, in accordance with international law, granted her permission to remain for twenty-four hours until 8 p.m. on December 2, 1939, while repairs were effected.

Nothing could have exceeded the kindness and consideration which the captain of the *Triad* received from the Norwegian authorities. The Norwegian shipbuilders excelled themselves, and six hours before the time was up the *Triad* steamed out of Norwegian territorial waters and set her course for home.

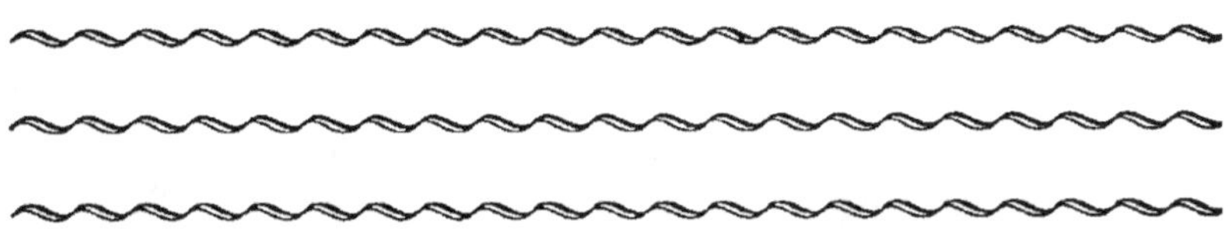

BEGINNER'S LUCK

IF EVER there was a case of Beginner's Luck, it was that of Lieutenant-Commander Maurice Kildare Cavenagh-Mainwaring, D.S.O., who, born in Staffordshire on April 13th, 1908, spent his youth in hunting and shooting, as though some instinct urged him to prepare for the much more serious hunting and shooting later on. Passing out of the Naval College at Dartmouth, which is set in such sylvan loveliness that the majority who go there leave it with a lasting impression of the beauty of England, he became a midshipman in the Royal Navy in 1925. Ambitious to command his own ship and eager to accept responsibility, he realized that the finest opportunity to achieve his desire lay in the submarine service. Accordingly he volunteered for this special branch of the navy in 1930 and in the ensuing years garnered all the experience that Peace could bring him. At the outbreak of war he served in a big ship in the Mediterranean, but he returned to England to join a submarine flotilla at a base on the east coast of England.

Some months later he was watching the builders put the finishing touches to His Majesty's submarine *Tuna*, which he was to command. Knowing what he wanted, he had worked to attain it, and had achieved his desire. So this officer with the blue eyes and wavy auburn hair found himself the captain of his ship for the second time at an early age. Slightly less than six feet tall, he has a ready smile for a quip and is blessed with the ability to see a joke when it is against himself.

He put the *Tuna* through her trials to see what she could do. "I think you had better go out and have a shake-down patrol to get used to the boat," said Captain Menzies, the captain of his flotilla. "We'll send you to a safe area for a five day patrol."

"All right, sir," was the reply, and at twilight one evening the captain of the *Tuna* left his base for his first war patrol. The crew were not yet shaken down, but they started to adjust themselves to the topsy-turvy meal times of the submarine routine which saw them sitting down to supper in the ward-room about 6 o'clock in the morning before diving. All day the *Tuna* went ahead on her motors beneath the surface, and a few minutes before midnight she came up to recharge and have the first meal of their day, or rather, night.

Lieutenant-Commander   Cavenagh-Mainwaring

was sitting in the wardroom having breakfast when Petty-Officer Morton, who was one of the look-outs, saw a dim light through his binoculars. It simply flashed and vanished. Concentrating on the spot, he saw it again thirty seconds later, and again it vanished. "It was like someone using a dimmed torch," he said afterwards. Keeping his glasses focused on the spot, he at length detected the conning-tower of a submarine that resembled a Dutch submarine with which they had sailed in company. Meanwhile the officer of the watch, Lieutenant W. N. R. Knox, had also identified the craft as a submarine.

The high-pitched buzz of the night alarm—very distinct from the lower note of the diving Klaxon—sounded through the boat. The captain of the *Tuna* quickly climbed the metal rungs of the conning-tower ladders to the bridge. It was a fairly dark night, and the sudden transition from the light of the wardroom to the darkness outside made it difficult for him to see until his eyes grew accustomed to the change.

"I can see a German submarine on the starboard bow, sir," said the first lieutenant.

The captain of the *Tuna* blinked at the velvety darkness. He could see nothing. "Will you take charge until I can see?" he said. "Alter course towards and up on a ninety track," he added, peering through his binoculars in an effort to locate the submarine.

"Coming on pretty close to firing time," said the first lieutenant, keeping his eyes on the enemy.

"I see him!" said the captain, just managing to

pick up a darker patch in the black expanse. His instructions for setting the torpedoes went down the voice pipe.

Three minutes after the night alarm had sounded, he gave the order to fire the torpedoes. They hissed off into the darkness toward the black shape nearly two miles away.

"Bring number one and two tubes to the ready," ordered the captain. He turned to the look-outs and the officer of the watch. "Get below," he ordered. Slipping after them through the conning-tower hatch, he swung the hatch down and pressed the button which set the Klaxon blaring to warn the crew to dive. Nearly two minutes had passed since he had fired—and two minutes is a long time to wait when nerves are taut. Feeling quite sure he had missed the target, he was just stepping off the lower rungs of the conning-tower ladder into the control room when there was a loud explosion.

He had sunk his first U-boat. Comprehension swept away the nervous tension.

Blowing the tanks, the captain of the *Tuna* surfaced, to have a look round. Not that he saw anything, for it was much too dark. But the strong smell of fuel oil which rose from the sea penetrated right through the boat and confirmed that the U-boat would go hunting no more.

It was indeed Beginner's Luck—the *Tuna* on her first patrol and the captain in his first wartime command. The peculiar thing was that for a fortnight previously many British submarines had been hunting in that area without sighting a single ship.

Next night, about the same time, the captain of the *Tuna* was swinging on to the ladder to go up to the bridge, when the diving hooter brought the look-outs and the officer of the watch rushing down as the *Tuna* started a crash dive. It was another U-boat coming straight at the *Tuna*, whose captain heard it pass within a hundred yards of them. The captain of the flotilla had certainly chosen a nice quiet spot in which to give the crew of the *Tuna* their first war experience.

Just after surfacing at dusk on the fifth night, the officer of the watch saw his third U-boat dive ahead. At once the captain took charge and there followed a desperate game of hide and seek between the antagonists—far more desperate than the captain of the *Tuna* was able to realize at the time. Very circumspectly he moved through the seas, waiting for a chance to get in a shot at the enemy; but the captain of the U-boat proved to be as wary as the captain of the *Tuna* and dodged about without giving the British captain an opening.

For hour after hour the German U-boat and the British submarine moved stealthily, seeking to destroy each other. More than once the captain of the *Tuna* thought that he had lost the U-boat completely, and just when it seemed that the hunt had been in vain the hydrophone operator picked up the noise of the U-boat and the hunt went on again.

For five or six hours the chase went on. Then the patience of the captain of the *Tuna* was rewarded with a chance to attack. He gave instructions to the men waiting by the torpedo tubes, and in a few seconds the torpedoes sped away after their quarry.

Almost at the same moment the hydrophone operator heard a most menacing sound growing louder in his earphones. "A torpedo coming straight at us, sir!" he said, excitedly.

Looking round quickly from the bridge, the captain saw the track of a torpedo overtake the *Tuna* and pass down the port side, while the men in the control room waited in suspense.

"Another torpedo coming straight at us, sir!" repeated the hydrophone operator, as the other men, all keyed-up, wondered how long it would be before the explosion came.

"Another torpedo coming straight at us—they're coming! they're coming! they're coming!" shouted the hydrophone operator in his excitement, making the suspense of the crew almost unbearable.

The captain on the bridge looked aft in the direction from which the other torpedo had come, and saw the tracks of three more torpedoes rushing down upon them to hurl them into eternity. Summing up their angle of approach in a glance, he barely had time to make a quick alteration of the helm to swing the *Tuna* off her course before the torpedoes passed harmlessly down the starboard side and vanished in the distance.

It was indeed a lucky escape, for the captain of the *Tuna* was blissfully unaware of the fact that two U-boats were operating in company, and while he was hunting one, the other was carefully stalking him. Had the operator been a trifle slower in reporting the torpedoes, and the captain a little hesitant in altering helm, there might have been one of those brief messages, "One of our submarines has failed to return."

But it was Beginner's Luck right to the end of that patrol, with enough excitement to blood the crew properly.

The next time the captain of the *Tuna* went on patrol he searched for a week before being called to the periscope by the welcome news that an enemy ship was in sight. He stalked her cunningly until he was within close range, when he promptly sank her with his torpedoes. A couple of nights later the *Tuna* was recharging on the surface under a bright moon when the night alarm buzzed and the captain made out a merchantman some miles away with an escort of two destroyers—an escort which plainly indicated that the ship was of major importance to the Axis confederates. At that distance, however, it was an open question whether he could succeed in getting close enough to deal with her. Speeding up, he did his best to close the range for fourteen minutes, by which time he felt sure that if he did not attack at once, she would probably draw off and escape. She was five miles away—a very long shot—

and the most skilful submariner in the world will acknowledge that it is good shooting to hit a ship at such a distance.

But the luck of the captain held. She steamed steadily on her set course while the *Tuna's* torpedoes raced after her. Nearly seven minutes later one overtook her and halted her for good.

By then the *Tuna* was fully submerged and doing her best to get as far as possible from the escorting destroyers, which lost little time in coursing down the torpedo tracks to drop their depth charges.

Skilfully evading the hunters, the captain of the *Tuna* raised his periscope to see what had happened to the ship. "I saw her with her bow sticking up in the air and the destroyers standing by picking up survivors, and about ten minutes afterwards she went down stern first. I thought then that we had got well away and could relax, when to my horror I saw the destroyers suddenly turn and come straight toward me. Just when they were getting too close to be pleasant, they altered course again and went back to the French coast."

The ship which Lieutenant-Commander M. K. Cavenagh-Mainwaring sank was heading out into the Atlantic; but whether she was an armed merchant cruiser or a submarine supply ship remains unknown.

His successes were marked by the award of the D.S.O., as well as by three treasured telegrams of congratulation from Admiral Sir Max Horton.

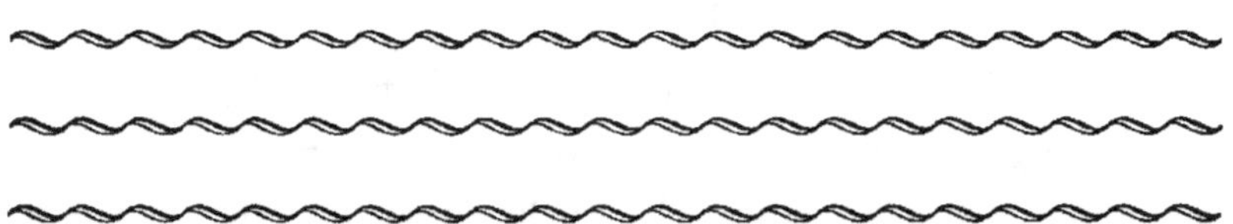

15

THE *SEALION'S* ADVENTURES

WELL over six feet tall, with dark eyes and hair and a wiry figure, Commander Benjamin Bryant, D.S.C., who was born on September 16, 1905, and went through Osborne and Dartmouth, has had some remarkable adventures since he took out the *Sealion* on her first patrol, early in 1940, when it was so cold and snowed so often that for three days his gun was buried under a mound of ice. Sailors know that the best way to thaw out frozen hawsers is to soak them in the sea, the temperature of which in winter is always higher than that of the air. On this occasion the sea was two degrees above freezing point, yet diving all day failed to melt the block of ice in which the gun and mounting were encased like a fly in amber.

No one inquires what happens if men fall ill on a submarine; but Commander Bryant found out on that trip. A submarine does not carry a doctor, so in emergencies the captain is expected to act as medical officer. He has a medicine chest, first aid outfits and a concise guide describing the symptoms of various diseases, and with these added to his own good sense he must do his best until he reaches port.

Many men shut up together in a submarine all day under the sea provide ideal theoretical conditions for spreading germs. It is a fine tribute to the general health of the men and the scientific care devoted to keeping them fit that illness is so rare. However, in bitter weather when the gun was locked up in that block of ice, Commander Bryant was suddenly called upon to fight germs instead of Germans. One of the men reported sick, with inflamed eyes and a bad headache. When the captain took his temperature, he found it was over 100 degrees fahrenheit.

Influenza had broken out in the ship. Man after man went down; one officer, then a second developed it. By the end of the day the *Sealion* was more like a hospital ship than a submarine, with eleven men and two officers on the sick list. All had aching heads, aching eyes, aching backs and high temperatures that in one case rose to 103.8. The usually happy *Sealion* felt far from happy. Three out of the four engine-room artificers went sick at the same time, and the outbreak threw a great strain on the rest of the crew.

Fighting the epidemic most ably with the simplest remedies, the captain found that the best treatment consisted of two aspirins and two Dover tablets—the latter being the remedy of Dampier's cut-throat companion, Dr. Dover, who proved that a bad man may still do some good in the world centuries after he is dead. These drugs, as often as required, soon started the men sweating, and in a couple of days most of them had thrown off the attack. Even the ill-wind which laid low the engine-room staff blew some good, for it suggested to the captain an improvement for preventing the watch-keepers from standing in a continual rush of cold air, which induced colds. It shows how his brain worked to improve the service.

One day an aircraft attacked the *Sealion* as she was moving at 45 feet below the surface. Three or four bombs broke a few lamps and gauge glasses, not to mention a rum glass, but the only man who felt sore about it was the seaman who got a bang on the head from a falling drip pan.

Another time he took the *Sealion* into the Skagerrak to stir up trouble and compel the Germans to chain down strong patrols of defensive craft in that area. After doing his damnedest, he stole away as secretly as possible, leaving the enemy defences on tenderhooks under the impression that he was still lurking about. As he departed, making his way through a German minefield for the second time in two days, he smiled happily as he heard the distant rumbles of depth charges miles away.

"We hoped these were in honour of *Sealion*," he remarked afterwards.

Despite his cleverness at the controls, the *Sealion* sometimes played weird tricks upon him in those waters, due to the different densities of the sea water and the layers of fresh water from the melting snows. One day the *Sealion* refused to stay on the bottom, but persisted in floating off because of a marked increase in the density of the sea-water which made her more buoyant than usual.

On more than one occasion in that patrol the *Sealion* fairly laughed at his efforts to make her dive deep. It was fantastic. She was like a fractious horse refusing to take a fence. After being trimmed, she would go down to a certain depth beyond which she would not budge. She came up against a dense layer, which might have been a solid road so far as she was concerned, for to push her nose through it was like trying to push it through the seabed, and she needed tons of extra ballast to overcome this abnormal condition of the sea. On the other hand, it had this advantage, that it was possible to take the *Sealion* along on top of this layer all day without adjusting the hydroplanes, as though she were indeed moving along the surface of a solid road. This matter of density touches the realm of paradox in the Dead Sea, where continual evaporation has made the chemical content of the water so dense that it is impossible for a man to sink at all, and a non-swimmer would find it difficult to commit suicide.

There was a morning when the *Sealion* started to go her own way in opposition to the captain's desires. With her helm altered hard a starboard, the captain noted with surprise that her bow began to swing to port. Ten, twenty, thirty degrees she swung and could not be checked. She swung more than half way round the compass, over 200 degrees, until she was pointing on the direct course for home, like a horse that has done its day's work and is anxious to get back to the stable. It was very mysterious and reminded Commander Bryant of the story of Balaam's ass in the Bible. The *Sealion* was actually trapped in a tidal rip that was too strong for her to overcome, and the force of the tide and the force of her propellers reached a stalemate, or balanced each other, when her nose was pointed towards home.

More than one British submarine captain has found that he could not stem the current and was drifting steadily backward while going submerged at full speed ahead. In ordinary times these abnormal conditions of current and densities are disconcerting, but in war they are dangerous. At any moment the captain of a submarine may be forced to dive to escape, and if he cannot make the depth he is vulnerable to the enemy, so while these physical conditions add to the interest of the submarine captain's life, they also add considerably to the risk, for if the boat refuses to behave in a normal manner in an emergency, the few seconds wasted in countering the abnormal conditions may make all the difference between destruction and escape.

To deal with difficulties created by the differences in densities, Commander Bryant was once compelled to jettison a tank full of distilled water in order to trim the *Sealion* properly. Next day the conditions compelled him to jettison nearly all the water in the freshwater tank, leaving barely enough for cooking and drinking.

"No water must be used for washing," he ordered.

The grimy faces and hands of officers and crew convinced him that the order was being obeyed. But two or three days after the ban was imposed he saw a sailor with clean hands. "Don't you know there is an order against washing?" he asked.

"Yes, sir," was the reply.

"Why are your hands clean?" said the captain.

"I haven't been washing, sir—I've just been rolling the bully beef rissoles," explained the sailor.

It was the perfect alibi.

Not until a week later, when they were on their way home, could the captain relax his restrictions. They all enjoyed their wash and brush up that morning.

The work on that patrol was beset with difficulties, groping about in the dark without any of the usual navigation lights by which to fix the position, dodging trawlers, as he put it, "to prevent being trawled up," so that some days it was necessary to take evasion action all round the clock. The strain can be imagined, but it made no difference to his sense of humour. One day a suspected conning-tower loomed upon the horizon. Travelling at full speed on the surface to close the target, he dived and worked into position while the torpedoes were prepared, and then "carried out a most spirited attack on the lug sail of a fishing boat," as he put it. Needless to add, the attack was terminated before the torpedoes were fired.

The days which liner passengers would call heavenly were to him and other submarine captains hellish, with calm seas that would enable the feather of the periscope to reel out its white warning and "v" ripples to any ship in sight and make plain to patrolling aircraft the sinister shape of the submarine below the surface. What Commander Bryant and his companions in the submarine service termed lovely submarine weather was a sea with plenty of chop on it which split up the outline of the submarine from the air and made it difficult to detect the periscope owing to the whole surface being broken up into blobs of high lights and shadows.

On April 11th, the third day of unfavourable submarine weather in succession, when the sea in the morning was, in the words of the captain, "mirror calm," the *Sealion*, after holding up a neutral steamer and allowing it to proceed, was hunted by some anti-submarine trawlers. She shook them off and went hunting herself about 4 o'clock in the afternoon, by which time a useful chop had developed on the sea. The captain wanted badly to go deep to increase his speed, but the density layers prevented him. The *Sealion* took about three-quarters of an hour to get within striking distance, and on signalling for the periscope to be raised Commander Bryant saw that an enemy seaplane was escorting a ship steaming at nine knots and flying the Nazi flag.

Just before 5 o'clock he fired his torpedoes. A minute later a torpedo hit the afterhold and the ship started to settle at once. The captain saw the bow rear up out of the sea and her stern slide under. When he last saw her, she was resting on the bottom with her bow sticking out of the water. That was the end of the *August Leonhart*.

Never were the audacity and grit of the captain and crew of the *Sealion* displayed more strongly than in that patrol. Night after night they were disturbed by air patrols, anti-submarine craft or fishing vessels and forced to dive before they could complete the recharging of their batteries. All on board were thankful about 4 o'clock one morning when the batteries were fully charged for the first time in six days. That afternoon, through the clearing rain, a convoy of six ships with an escort of nine trawlers was sighted, and Commander Bryant promptly prepared to attack. But the periscope was so fogged by rain that the image could not be seen properly to obtain the correct range. The hum of the *Sealion's* motors under water was picked up by the enemy trawler escorts, who warned the steamers to alter course in time to avoid the torpedoes which were fired.

At once a flying-boat pounced down to attack the submarine while two of the trawlers hastened to the spot. Two depth charges dropped by the flying-boat overhead were unpleasantly close, as the captain started to take the *Sealion* deeper. There came another explosion, the surge of which started to sweep the submarine toward the surface as though she were a chip of wood. To avoid disaster, the captain at once flooded all tanks to carry her down and put the motors at full speed to regain control. Anyone who has been brought to a standstill by an eighty or ninety miles gale which it was impossible to face will know what the captain and crew felt like when their massive ship was caught up like a toy.

Their trim, that delicate balance which enabled them to go up or down on the motors simply by altering the angle of the hydroplanes, was completely lost. All that the captain strove to do was to keep her under and take her deep.

"Some interesting moments occurred before the boat was stopped at 30 feet," he admitted later—one of those glorious understatements by which so many submarine captains dismiss their danger and conceal their valour and efficiency.

Another two depth charges exploded and shook them. "Meanwhile the hunting craft came up and started in with quite good shots," he added impersonally.

They had a bad quarter of an hour and switchbacked up and down in the most erratic manner while Lieutenant H. R. B. Newton strove to regain the trim and get her under control. The hydrophones were knocked out by the shock, which prevented them from keeping track of their hunters, but after an exciting sixteen minutes, during which all stood quietly carrying out orders and watching the dials of their instruments, Lieutenant Newton regained trim by blowing some of the ballast from tanks which had no gauges to guide him, as they had been put out of action. While he was using his skill to bring this about, the enemy dropped eleven more depth charges.

The *Sealion* started to crawl slowly away, altering course from time to time to hoodwink the hunters. The depth charges continued to explode, some of them very close. There was nothing haphazard about the attacks. They were, in the words of the captain, well organized.

The crew were quite unmoved. "There are nine trawlers with ten depth charges each," said the captain to his crew. "You can amuse yourselves by counting how many more are to come." So the word was passed through the boat and one of the crew kept a tally of the charges as they exploded. They had faith in their captain, in their boat, and in themselves and they were unafraid.

"What did you do in the control room?" Commander Bryant was asked.

"The conversation hinged around the effect of the curfew, which had been announced in the press, and on the sporting facilities of Brighton," was the reply.

That conveys a graphic picture of the superb courage of the men in the submarine service. In deadly danger, stealing slowly away in the depths to try to save their ship and their lives, they could chat as idly as though they were drinking a tankard of ale in an old English inn. The fact that water was leaking into the boat did not disturb them. It was a very leaky gland, but the chief engine-room artificer got the measure of it by organizing a line of men to pass buckets of water from the engine-room to the after bilge. They escaped some three hours later, to sight a tanker which the captain hoped would prove ample recompense for missing the convoy, but his luck was out. A rain squall obscured the tanker which changed course and vanished.

Just after 11 o'clock at night the *Sealion* came to the surface off one of the fiords. Her batteries were very low, and preparations were at once made to blow out the ship and recharge. One of the main Diesel engines was started up, the propeller de-clutched to disconnect it, and the clutch slipped in to turn the motor into a dynamo for recharging the giant batteries. Five minutes after the engine started to run, the captain sighted an enemy bomber emerging from a cloud. He did not wait. As he pulled the conning-tower hatch after him he saw the aircraft turn toward the *Sealion*. With only one motor and propeller in action and little power in the batteries, he took longer than usual to dive. The needle of the depth meter pointed to no more than 40 feet when a bomb exploded close amidships on the starboard side, there was a slight lag before another exploded on the port side.

"These were good bombs," he once said, with the scientific detachment of a born submarine officer.

The lights went out, the gyroscopic compass ceased to function along with the hydroplanes and a few air leaks developed in the high pressure system, but the repair of these defects was soon put in hand.

Sixty-eight minutes after the *Sealion* dived her captain once more surfaced. That was at 12.23 a.m. on the following morning. A minute later an enemy aircraft roared down on them and forced them to dive again. The hunt was on with a vengeance. The captain was caught with low batteries which robbed him of his power to crash dive and get clear if he was attacked while he was recharging on the surface.

All he could do was to use the remaining electrical power to steal away as far as possible and remain down until it was safe to surface and recharge.

The gyroscopic and magnetic compasses were upset by the bombing, with the result that although Commander Bryant set course to the west, the *Sealion* moved to the south-west.

For hour after hour she crawled away ever so slowly. About midday the captain stopped her on a layer at 45 feet. Layers had often created difficulties for him, but this was a boon, for it enabled the *Sealion* to remain stationary as though she were floating on the surface. The boat was in absolute darkness. The crew lay about. The air grew fouler. By the afternoon heads began to ache. It was indeed a long day. They lay there dozing in the dark, just waiting for nightfall, so that they could surface, and get some fresh air into their lungs and more power into their batteries.

From time to time fresh supplies of a chemical that absorbs carbon-dioxide were used to regenerate the air—when human beings breathe in oxygen to keep the human machine running, the waste gas which they expel is carbon-dioxide, or carbonic acid gas. The fact that soda lime absorbs carbon-dioxide was used by Fluess at the beginning of the century as the basis of his invention of a portable diving dress to enable divers to dispense with air pipes when engaged on certain work, and I have myself been under water for a considerable time testing a metal diving dress in which I breathed air that was regenerated by expelling the breath through a bag of soda lime to rob it of the dangerous carbon-dioxide which, if it rises above a certain small percentage—about 4 per cent.—causes death. The victims in the Black Hole of Calcutta and in the tragic *Thetis* disaster were all poisoned by carbon-dioxide.

About 5 o'clock in the afternoon the captain ordered a bottle of oxygen to be released. This brought the men relief and swept away their drowsy feelings. Three more hours dragged by, and they heard the sounds of distant explosions. As the hands of the clock crept round to 10.16 p.m. they heard the powerful explosions of depth charges moderately close.

The hunters were still on their track. Commander

Bryant had no illusions on this score. The question was whether the hunters would give up the hunt before the *Sealion* was forced to the surface by lack of air. By then the position was growing desperate.

A quarter of an hour later the hydrophone operator heard a trawler hunting for them. Backward and forward it moved for what seemed an age, starting up and stopping while the *Sealion* with her crew of exhausted men hung on grimly, floating on that layer at 45 feet below the surface.

"She's going off, sir," reported the hydrophone operator at 11 o'clock.

They were saved.

But Commander Bryant was too prudent to bring the *Sealion* to the surface yet. There was too much risk. They had been down so long and their position was so desperate that it was vital to blow out the boat and recharge without being disturbed, so he waited until he felt sure the coast was clear, and then at 11.50 p.m. he surfaced.

Directly the conning-tower hatch was open and the fresh air began to enter their lungs, every man on board was sick, owing to the physical condition brought about by their long dive. Some of them had not eaten for thirty hours, for although some cold food and lime juice were served about twelve hours earlier, none of them felt like eating.

"We were fortunate," stated the captain. "I do not think we could have stayed down much longer. We had been down forty-five hours except seven minutes."

Two or three hours later their headaches wore off, and next day they were on patrol as keen as ever. Before the end of that patrol, in order to ensure the total destruction of a ship which was ashore, he fired a torpedo at her. "I did not molest the local coastal traffic with gunfire. Without affecting the progress of the war, it seemed to me that it was more likely to alienate the feelings of the local Norwegians as well as disclosing our position. It was hoped that the torpedo hitting the wreck would be put down to some other cause," he commented with dry humour.

It was the custom of Commander Bryant to hold divine service every Sunday in the control room and he insisted on the attendance of all the officers and men, no matter what denomination they professed. These services were held at any convenient time, and it was a common spectacle to see the officer of the watch with his eye glued to the periscope searching the seas for enemy ships while he lustily joined in a hymn or said "Amen" to a prayer.

After the service, Commander Bryant used to preach a little sermon and tell them what they had done wrong in their drills the previous week and how they could remedy these shortcomings and improve their team work. He always finished by telling the crew the plan for the following week and describing the object of their patrols so that each man would know what he was doing and why he was doing it.

Some members of the crew, after a spell of duty, were not too pleased at having to get out of their bunks to attend the service and they would much rather have gone without their sermons than their sleep. When the captain called the crew to prayers one Sunday the prayer book could not be found and he was forced to abandon the service.

The following week was one of the worst the crew ever experienced, everything went wrong, torpedoes missed, aircraft dropped bombs on them, and it culminated in that grim hunt which kept them under for nearly two days.

The next Sunday Commander Bryant for the first time in his experience saw all the crew voluntarily assemble in the control room without receiving the usual order for prayers, and directly he stepped in, the missing prayer book was presented to him. Someone had "found" it again, but where it was hidden and who managed to find it, the captain was too wise to inquire.

After that the whole crew of the *Sealion* reckoned it would bring bad luck not to hold the Sunday service, a view which was strengthened next day when a convoy was sighted and three of their torpedoes secured hits.

On another patrol the *Sealion* was out again in Norwegian waters on a patrol which brought her to the edge of disaster and proved once more the outstanding courage and efficiency of Commander Bryant and his crew. There was, however, a pleasant interlude on a beautiful morning before that ordeal. The captain was carefully examining the shore of a fiord when he suddenly saw the windows of a house thrown wide open by a charming blond who proceeded to do her morning exercises in the nude before the window, quite unconscious of the watchful eye at the periscope. The captain was quite taken aback. No doubt the lady was equally surprised a little later to see a steamer suddenly sink in the fiord after a startling explosion—due to one of the *Sealion's* torpedoes.

Exploring two fiords, Commander Bryant sighted a convoy in the afternoon and at once manœuvred to intercept and attack. The convoy was protected by an escort of seven trawlers, two of which were camouflaged in cream and brown. Using all his guile to evade the trawlers, he was working slowly into position for a shot at a big ice-breaker in the van of the port line of the convoy when she changed course and presented an impossible target. Had Commander Bryant tried to move across her bow to get a shot on her starboard side he would have run right into some of the escorting trawlers. Accordingly he turned his attention to the other ships and was working into position to fire his torpedoes when he saw a small ship swing out of the line and drive straight at him to ram. Knowing that a dense layer would prevent him from diving deep and escaping, he sought to evade the oncoming ship by using his helm.

It was vain. The captain had barely raised the after periscope to see the position of the attacker when the keel of the ship struck the periscope standards and snapped them off. The *Sealion* reeled under the impact. Her crew were flung in all directions as she swung up in the white wake of the attacker. But the captain's prompt action prevented her from breaking surface. They were blinded by the blow, a ship without eyes, unable to see, but still able to hear what was going on. All wondered how badly the *Sealion* was damaged. The captain knew the periscopes had gone. He did not know what had happened to the bridge, whether the upper conning-tower was so damaged as to prevent the hatch from being opened—which would have been extremely awkward.

Flooding the main ballast tanks, he forced the *Sealion* deep and followed the convoy as being the safest course to pursue. Having heard nothing of the hunters for three-quarters of an hour, he decided to run the pump. Instantly the hydrophone operator heard two hunting craft approaching. They also had been lying low, listening, waiting for the *Sealion* to give away her position. They were wily, and Commander Bryant had the greatest difficulty in shaking them off. For five hours he pitted his skill against theirs before he escaped. Then, just after 11 o'clock that night, he brought the submarine to the surface, and to his delight found that the conning-tower hatch opened freely, and the bridge was undamaged.

A mass of tangled wire and wreckage met his eye. The standard in which the after periscope worked had been snapped clean through at the level of the deck. Had it not been for the periscope tube in which were assembled the thousand lenses which make up this wonderful instrument the standard would undoubtedly have been carried overboard, but the periscope sticking up inside the standard prevented it from going over the side, just as a sweep's brush sticking up through a chimney-pot would prevent a chimney from being blown over the chimney stack. As Commander Bryant afterwards remarked, the periscope must be marvelously tough.

The position of the forward standard was fraught with danger. It hung over the starboard side of the bridge, suspended by the jumping wire that was attached to the top of the broken after periscope standard. Every time the *Sealion* rolled, the forward standard swung hard against the side of the ship. Even the captain, who remained cool as ice in the face of every imaginable danger, was alarmed. The standard hanging over the side of the bridge swung about like a gigantic pendulum, crashing against the side, and threatening to crush the men on the bridge at any moment. So grave was the danger that the captain ordered everyone off the bridge for fear that they would be killed.

But if they were to survive, that swaying mass of

metal must be secured, it was essential to fasten it so that it would not damage the structure of the submarine. They were in a precarious situation. The enemy coast was near. At any moment the hunters might return to resume the chase. The *Sealion's* batteries were run down and had to be recharged. The *Sealion* was blinded by the loss of her periscopes if forced to dive, she could not speak to her base because her wireless aerials had been carried away.

Without delay the engine-room staff started up the main engines to recharge the batteries, while the rest of the crew strove to secure the broken periscope standards. Line after line was fastened to the swaying forward standard by grapnel and jigger, only to be snapped as the great mass swayed about in the heaving seas. That crisis brought an idea for giving the ship a list by taking water into some of the port tanks, so that when the *Sealion* heeled over to port, the swinging standard would come to rest against the starboard side of the ship. This brilliant notion was eventually carried out, and the movement of the forward standard was restricted for the time being. Then they set about lashing the snapped-off after standard securely to the mast.

Having carried out first aid to both standards, the crew of the submarine started to cut through the jumping wires to free the forward standard. It was a most difficult task that could only be attempted single-handed. The wire jerked and swayed with the movements of the ship, and a man had to perch up awkwardly amid the wreckage of the mast aerial and saw away with a hack saw at arm's length at this wire, which would not keep still. The tiring posture made it impossible for a man to work more than fifteen minutes at a time, and when one tired, another took over.

Suddenly one of the wires parted. Unfortunately the jerk was so great that it snapped the lashings, with the result that the forward standard again began to sway and crash against the plating.

Unable to remain on the surface longer for fear of being surprised, Commander Bryant was forced to dive. All day right up to 11 o'clock that night the *Sealion* groped her way under the sea. When she was brought to the surface an hour before midnight the sea was calmer and the crew were able to cut the forward standard adrift and clear up the wreckage. Petty Officer Clark, the wireless operator, exercised his ingenuity and ran considerable risk by rigging a new aerial from the forward Lewis gun standard to a position aft, while the seas were washing over the casing on which he secured a precarious foothold.

The *Sealion* was four days getting away from the scene of the attack and making her way across the North Sea—which the Germans grandiloquently call the German Ocean. The ship was crippled, but the crew remained undaunted by all the hazards they had endured and overcome. Once or twice enemy aircraft forced her to dive, but no Nazi warship dared venture forth to try to intercept her.

"My warm congratulations on your most determined and successful patrol," wired Sir Max Horton to Commander Bryant. "It was bad luck over the convoy. Now to enjoy your well-earned leave."

Faced with the necessity of spending Christmas on patrol, Commander Bryant decided to mark the festive season by taking some chickens for the Christmas dinner of officers and crew. In those days the *Sealion* had no refrigerator, and as she left base on December 22nd it was problematical whether the chickens would keep. The crew, watching their chickens carefully, concluded on December 24th that if they were not eaten at once they would not be fit to eat at all, so they anticipated their Christmas dinner by one day and thoroughly enjoyed the birds.

But the captain and officers were determined to have chicken for their Christmas dinner, and in order to preserve their fowl they stored it in the ballast pump bilge, which was considered the coolest place in the boat. Every evening when the first lieutenant went the rounds, he visited the bilge to take a sniff at the bird to see if it would hold out. To the delight of the ward-room, it did—but only just! It was a trifle gamey, but the officers were happy. They pulled their crackers, put on paper hats and smoked cigars. Afterwards the crew held races along the mess deck with mechanical toy motor cars; and they had a grand "uckers" competition between the various messes.

While millions of Britons were holding their festivities ashore, the crew of the *Sealion* held theirs under the sea during their daily hunt for enemy ships.

Despite the perils which beset them, they had their lighter moments, as when the officer of the watch said to a seaman: "How far are you off your course?"

The seaman, whose only previous sea experience had been as passenger on a ferry, replied: "About an inch, sir."

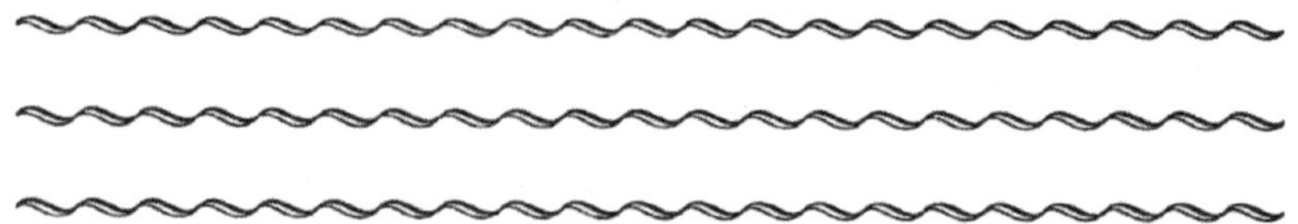

16

TRAPPED IN A MINEFIELD

No one could have been prouder than Lieutenant J. S. Huddart when he sailed from the east coast base in the H44, for she was his first command. Some naval men prefer destroyers, others lean toward cruisers or the big ships of the line, but it was the submarine service which cast its lure over Lieutenant Huddart. That is the way most men in the submarine service feel. The hardships and dangers which they know will surely be their lot seem to vanish before the spell exercised by the submarine service.

They have a saying: "Once a submarine man, always a submarine man," and from the affectionate way in which they talk of their ships and service it is largely true. But submarine work is necessarily that of the young man. It demands high physical fitness and calls for sound lungs and a stout heart. It appeals strongly to the officer with scientific leanings, one to whom the questions of balance and counterbalance and air pressures and water pressures and the capacity of pumps come easily. Where other men might find these subjects dull, he finds them full of fascination—as in fact they are. The pilot flying a bomber is not more highly trained than he, nor are the engines and electrical equipment in the aircraft so crowded and complicated as all the devices fitted into a submarine to enable men to live and sleep and move about under the sea.

During his first war patrol Lieutenant Huddart got on good terms with his ship and learned her little foibles, how she answered the helm, how quickly she could crash dive in an emergency and how all the intricate machinery functioned. He knew her well, of course, before he took her out, for the Admiralty is not so crass as to send a submarine to sea in charge of a man who was not familiar with her. Indeed, a submarine officer may stand by to watch a submarine being built, so that by the time she is finished he knows as much about her intricacies as any living man. Consequently when the H44 returned to base, her commander was satisfied that he understood her and had got the feel of her, just as a violinist gets the feel of a fiddle and settles down to a happy partnership.

As Lieutenant Huddart walked smartly over the quay to the H44 he had high hopes of a successful patrol. He had tested out his ship under war conditions and knew what she could do. Having studied his Admiralty instructions concerning courses, the movements of certain naval units and other vital information in his secret orders, he was anxious to start.

Next day the H44 rolled continuously in a rough sea. The wind which at times touched nearly thirty miles an hour would have been regarded as half a gale by landsmen although sailormen would refer to it off-handedly as a stiff breeze. The submarine made heavy going of it. As she rolled, her gyro-compass swung to and fro so violently, and was pulled up so often with a jerk as it rocked, that it went completely mad. Instead of pointing steadily to the north, it wandered about in all directions and Lieutenant Huddart was obliged to steer her by guess work until he could take a sight of the stars. Even when he dived to ease the rolling, the gyro-compass still played tricks, and it was five hours before it got over its mad attack and settled down after misbehaving for nine hours. With all the aids of science, the navigation of a submarine is not easy; lacking a compass, it is fraught with dangers.

For the next five days Lieutenant Huddart continued his patrol without seeing a single target for his torpedoes. It was a normal patrol, with all the normal duties carried out with skill and care. The only thing lacking to touch it with excitement was an enemy ship as a target. Very early in the morning, while it was still dark, the H44 floated on the surface while her engines hummed rhythmically recharging her batteries. Dinner was prepared and eaten, the usual cup of tea consumed, and all the crockery washed and put away when Lieutenant Huddart sounded the hooter for diving stations just before dawn and took the submarine down to 45 feet, out there in the North Sea off the east coast of England. The watch was set, and two-thirds of the crew turned in to sleep after their day's work was done.

The hands of the clock pointed to five minutes to six in the morning and the steady hum of the motors droned through the ship. Suddenly something hit the port side of the ship and scraped its way along. The sound could be heard clearly above the drone of the motors. That it meant danger was sure; what form of danger the listeners could only imagine.

"Something scraping down the port side, sir," said the officer of the watch, rousing the captain. Instantly Lieutenant Huddart took control. Altering the hydroplanes, he took his ship down to 65 feet, hoping to escape the unknown danger. He queried the hydrophone operator whether any hydrophone effect had been heard to indicate a ship.

"No engine noises, sir," came the answer. "It sounded like a wire on the hull."

This ruled out the possibility of a ship sweeping for the British submarine, a possibility that was already negatived by his proximity to the English coast, for an enemy ship in that position in daylight could hardly hope to escape the attack of surface ships and aircraft. Lieutenant Huddart guessed the worst—that his ship had bumped into the cable of a mine. It could not have been anything else. An enemy submarine working surreptitiously in the dark must have laid a new minefield into which he had wandered, a minefield very cleverly sited.

Lieutenant Huddart did not turn a hair. His first reaction was to take the H44 deeper. It was the best reply to the danger. The fact that he had struck a cable proved that the mines were floating at a higher level, which suggested that the trap was set for surface ships. By going deeper he placed a wider margin of safety between his ship and the mines, although there was still the risk of running into the mooring cables. If, of course, the enemy had laid a special trap for submarines, with mines scattered about the deeper levels, it was a bad look-out indeed.

He moved forward slowly, hoping that the danger was past, but listening as keenly as the hydrophone operator for the faintest sound from outside. For fifteen minutes no other sound was heard but the hum of the motors. Then that dread scraping sound came again. It was forward, still on the port side of the ship, and just by the port wing of the hydroplane. The scraping was quickly followed by several dull bumps.

Lieutenant Huddart pushed the submarine ahead. This time there was no sound of a wire sliding away along the port side. Instead, the shafting of the fore hydroplanes started to jerk in a sickening manner. "Bump! Bump! Bump!" went something forward, interspersed with that ugly scraping on the hull.

It was now certain that the submarine had picked up some obstruction, but until Lieutenant Huddart had seen what caused the sounds, he could only assume what it was. It must be a mine, it could be nothing else. In his marrow he knew the sounds were the portents of death, yet he stood calmly in the control-room thinking out a way of escape.

He gave a quiet order, and the forward hydro-planes were gradually worked through their full limits. He stood listening, wondering. The sounds ceased. If the silence were anything to judge by, the working of the hydroplanes had apparently shaken off the obstruction. Yet he could not be sure. Her trim was all right. He could feel no sign of any weight forward that disturbed her balance.

Still he was not sure. But he intended to surface to find out. For all his outward calm, no man could endure that suspense without being concerned, but he masked his personal feelings as though nothing had happened at all.

Remembering that there was a swell running from the north, he very gently altered course to prevent the submarine rolling when she reached the surface. He had already experienced to the full how much she could roll and was determined not to take any unnecessary risk. If a mine were still entangled on her hull, the first roll she made was likely to detonate it. To bring her bow round to ride the swell while she was beneath the surface was a sensible pre-caution.

At 6.35 a.m. he started to turn her. She had been under helm barely two minutes when those terrifying sounds began again. They still came from forward, but were not on the port side this time. The scraping and bumping obviously came from the region of the starboard hydroplane.

"I must bring her up on an even keel," he decided.

The safety of the ship and all on board depended upon his skill. At 6.40 a.m. his quiet voice set the compressed air hissing along the air lines to expel the water from the ballast tanks. He did it very gradually, so that an equal weight was blown out of each tank. He knew that a jerk might mean the end of everything. Very slowly the submarine began to rise on a perfectly level keel until she reached 25 feet.

Then something began to bump heavily upon the starboard side. The men on duty waited. The tension was great.

Bringing the periscope into use the moment he reached periscope depth, the captain saw that he was towing a mine which was hung up about four feet from the stern. He could not make out whether it was caught on the starboard hydroplane or the rudder.

It seemed impossible for the H44 to escape destruction. It could only be a matter of seconds in the sway of the sea before one of the horns touched and blew them all to bits.

In the face of that dreadful danger, the courage

and resource of Lieutenant Huddart stood out brighter than ever. He was not prepared to wait for the sea to deal a death blow. The way to possible salvation flashed through his mind and he acted instantly. Speeding up, he swung her over to port in the hope of washing the mine off to starboard. For a minute it trailed along. Then as the wash and speed increased it broke away. That ordeal which lasted two minutes, must have seemed a lifetime. Directly he had shaken off the mine he began to regard it with a more tranquil eye. It was a wicked-looking sphere painted black, and as it rose on the swell he counted at least twelve horns round its circumference—twelve chances of death. How that mine managed to bump against the British submarine for half an hour without touching one of those horns was a mystery—and a miracle.

Having won safety for himself, he strove to ensure the safety of others by sinking the mine or exploding it, but in this the Lewis gunner failed.

The danger, however, was by no means over, for at 7.30 that morning he was proceeding very circumspectly on the surface when he saw a mine break surface in the swell to starboard at the same time that another was sighted four feet below the surface to port. By the grace of God he passed between them, with neither more than 25 feet away from his hull.

It was a providential escape. For ninety-five minutes the submarine had run the gauntlet of a minefield and had escaped scot free. Without delay Lieutenant Huddart plotted the course of his ship to fix the exact position in order to warn the Admiralty of the danger. Sights were taken to check its position and in order to make quite sure the captain of the submarine took soundings and got a fix ashore which enabled the sweepers to locate and deal with those mines.

One of the most amazing things in this amazing escape is that two-thirds of the crew had no idea what had happened. They slept through it all, for Lieutenant Huddart refused to disturb them. That decision marked not only his cool judgment in that crisis, but also his humanity and consideration. To rouse the sleeping men in order to subject them to all the hopes and fears suffered by the men on watch would have done no good and it was much more merciful to allow them to sleep.

"I consider this a sensible and cool-headed action," said the senior officer at the base. "This patrol promises well both for his ability and good fortune."

The officers and men on duty were aware that at any moment they might be blown to bits; their nervous tension must have been acute; yet they acted quite coolly throughout. "The behaviour of the ship's company during these operations was wholly admirable," stated Lieutenant Huddart, who later struck some telling blows at the Axis shipping, especially in the Mediterranean.

His hair-raising adventure of towing a live mine

recalls the adventure of Admiral M. E. Nasmith, V.C., who had a similar experience in making his way out of the Dardanelles in the last war. By brilliant seamanship he also cleared the mine and escaped, but it was not the sort of ordeal to undergo twice.

CRUSHED BY THE SEA

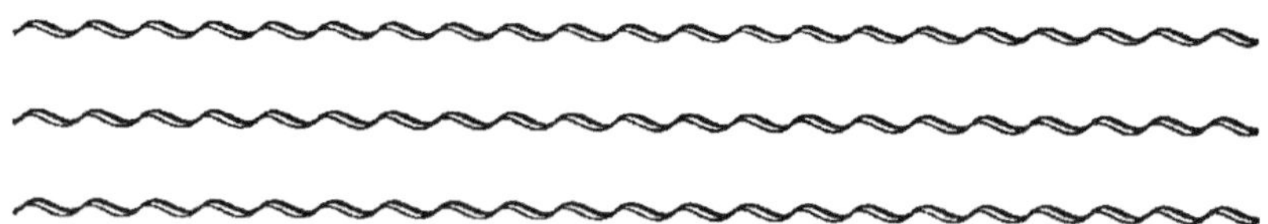

WHETHER the *Scharnhorst* is the luckiest or the unluckiest ship afloat depends upon the viewpoint. The Admiralty and the Air Ministry can adduce ample evidence to prove her good luck, yet this same evidence may be regarded by the Germans as proof of her bad luck. While the enemy can aver that she is always getting into trouble, the British naval and air authorities must admit that she is always getting out of it. How many shells, torpedoes and bombs have struck her without destroying her is known only to the enemy, but Mr. Winston Churchill announced in the House of Commons that the Royal Air Force dropped 4,000 tons of bombs in an attempt to destroy her and the *Gneisenau* and *Prinz Eugen* in Brest harbour and a ship that survives such an appalling bombardment must surely be counted as lucky, as she was to escape with her consorts through the Straits of Dover.

Her lives are apparently as numerous as her watertight compartments. How many compartments she is divided into is another mystery, but judging by the times she has been struck without going to the bottom, she would appear to be more of a honeycomb than a ship.

Naval architects have striven for years to construct the unsinkable ship, but the technical developments in the *Scharnhorst* seem to have been carried a stage further than in British naval ships of a similar class and date. At the same time it is well to remember that the Germans trumpeted over the world that their great new battleship *Bismarck* was unsinkable from sea or air, and there is no doubt that every technical refinement which the Germans could think of was incorporated into her, yet the Royal Navy disembowelled her and sent her to the bottom of the Atlantic. This suggests that the unsinkable ship has yet to be built and that the *Scharnhorst* must have been lucky indeed.

The *Renown* caught her first with a few big shells during the Nazi invasion of Norway. But she had the speed of the *Renown* and made her escape, to vanish from the ken of the Royal Navy for some weeks. Rumours that she hid away in a secret spot on the northern coast of Norway while repairs were made, were not confirmed officially, and the Royal Navy, as ever, remained silent.

Yet the Navy had its eyes ever on the watch, among them the eyes of Lieutenant-Commander D. Ingram who, leaving his base in June, 1940, moved stealthily along the Norwegian coast, peering through the periscope of the *Clyde*, waiting and watching for a chance to strike at the enemy. The *Clyde* was one of the big ocean-going submarines of the Royal Navy, with 1,500 tons displacement and a speed of 22 knots on the surface. Capable of travelling thousands of miles without refuelling, she could remain at sea for weeks if necessary. Long patrols, however, are not good policy. The topsy-turvy life of the crew who seldom see daylight from the time they leave base until they return is itself unnatural; the main meal as already stated is generally eaten when the men would normally be asleep. Such conditions are inseparable from life in a submarine. They impose a strain on the men. The risks of war and the demands of high technical efficiency increase the strain. It is essential that the men be always at concert pitch. To ensure this extra alertness and efficiency the spell of duty is reduced to two hours, instead of the four hours served by the naval men in surface ships, with a rest period lasting four hours.

Experience has shown that a man tends to tire after concentrating for two hours—anyone who has waited and watched intently while the hand of a clock moved around five minutes can imagine what it means to watch a dial or depth gauge for two hours on end, as the crew of a submarine have to do when they are running submerged, for upon their dials and gauges depends their very existence and any variations must be noted and corrected instantly. Hence the short spells of concentration and the long spells of relaxation.

Out of an overcast Norwegian sky on the evening of June 5th trouble roared down on the *Clyde* while she was recharging her batteries, for under cover of the cloud a Heinkel 111 stole up astern and was not sighted, owing to the bad visibility, until within two miles. The hooter sounded through the boat and the *Clyde* dived, but before she could vanish the enemy had covered the intervening two miles at top speed and swept over the top of the submarine, spraying her with bullets and cannon shells. When the danger was past, the captain of the *Clyde* found that three holes two and a half inches in diameter had been shot through the steel plating of the bridge. It was lucky the holes were not through the pressure hull. But what annoyed him was that he had given away his position to the Nazis, who were warned that a British submarine was lurking about. Extra watchfulness on the part of the foe meant a diminished chance of the *Clyde* sinking something big.

From that time onward the area was so carefully patrolled by aircraft that the *Clyde* was unable to move along the surface. Directly she attempted to do so, an aircraft came along and forced her under. In such conditions it was no easy matter to recharge batteries, and on one occasion the battery was so run down that the captain was obliged to go well out to sea in order to remain undisturbed by the aircraft patrolling the coast. That big ships were at sea he learned on the afternoon of June 10th when he sighted the masts of a pocket battleship and a cruiser of the *Hipper* class. But they were too far off for him to get within striking range although he strove to keep in touch by sending the *Clyde* full speed ahead on the surface. The enemy drew away and in fifteen minutes had passed from sight.

Early next morning, just before 7 o'clock, another big enemy ship was sighted, quite beyond the reach of the *Clyde*. So the days and nights passed in waiting, watching and hoping.

A rough sea and a strong wind ushered in June 20th. By 9 o'clock in the morning the seas were running so high that it was impossible to see at periscope depth owing to the waves obscuring the periscope. To see over the tops of the waves it was necessary to come to the surface. As the day wore on the sea grew rougher and the wind increased. All day the *Clyde* patrolled, keeping watch in these difficult conditions, and about 8 o'clock that night the captain took her to the surface to recharge the batteries. For nearly two hours the task continued without interruption. Then, just before 10 o'clock, an aircraft was seen and the *Clyde* slid out of sight and steered toward the north.

Within twenty minutes the alarm passed through the ship. About eight miles away, at the extreme range of visibility, some ships were detected against the dark background. They were indistinct, but in a few minutes the captain of the *Clyde* made them out through the spray and spume as two capital ships and a destroyer. The two big ships were steaming abreast about two miles apart, with the destroyer screening them ahead. A wind touching 30 miles an hour whipped the tops off the seas. The periscopes were so often blotted out by the water that the captain was forced to bring the *Clyde* up until the periscope standards were awash in order to observe the enemy. Her liveliness in the heavy seas made her so difficult to manage that tons of extra ballast had to be shipped to trim her and prevent her from breaking surface. Even so she could not be controlled except at full speed.

The captain noted with delight that the enemy ships were approaching him, so this time there would be no difficulty in closing his target. Seeking to check the range, he was quite unable to fix the waterline of the ships owing to the rough seas. As the minutes went, and he issued orders for setting and timing the torpedoes, he identified the further ship as a pocket battleship, while the ship which he was working into position to attack was apparently the battle cruiser *Scharnhorst*. It was then too late for him to attempt to alter his target and attack the pocket battleship. The *Clyde* was bucketing in the swell and continuous action was needed to prevent her from surging to the surface. "I was so afraid of breaking the surface," he stated afterwards, "a catastrophe which was but narrowly averted several times."

Her emergence above the surface for a second would have robbed him of his chance to punish the enemy.

Twenty minutes after first sighting the ships, Lieutenant-Commander Ingram had manœuvred the *Clyde* to avoid the destroyer and gain a position for a clean shot at the *Scharnhorst*, which was doing twenty knots. She was two and a quarter miles away when he steadied his ship at 10.32 p.m. and gave the order to fire.

"Torpedoes running, sir," reported the hydrophone operator, as the torpedoes sped through the sea.

The captain wondered if the explosion would never come. There are so many slips in the submarine service that anything is possible. But exactly 2 minutes 55 seconds after firing the first torpedo there was a violent explosion. "It seemed like a double explosion, a less violent sort of echo following a second later," the captain subsequently remarked. He listened eagerly for more explosions, but all that the hydrophone operator heard were the faint explosions of the other torpedoes hitting the seabed some eight minutes later.

To prevent the *Clyde* from bobbing like a cork to the surface after the torpedoes were fired—a torpedo weighs over a ton—Lieutenant F. E. Macvie took in even more ballast, and a few seconds after the big explosion occurred he altered the hydroplanes to force her deep to avoid the enemy's counter-attack. The *Clyde* was out of trim, and those tons of extra ballast taken in to prevent her from swinging to the surface now carried her down steeply. Down she went. Lieutenant Macvie tried to check her dive and straighten her out. He failed. She continued to dive and all his efforts with the hydroplanes could not stop her. He watched the depth gauge on which the coxswain's eyes were fixed—and still the needle kept moving. Would it ever stop? Or would she continue to sink until the pressure of the sea crushed the steel hull like cardboard?

The limit to which a submarine can dive is fixed by her designers who build her to withstand the pressures at that depth. A safety margin is provided, but to dive much beyond her limit is to dive to destruction.

The *Clyde* was well down in the danger zone, in the grip of deadly pressures, when she was at length pulled up with her stern fifty feet lower than her bow. The implacable sea strove to crush her flat. This was no figment of the imagination, but the simple truth. The average person who has never undergone abnormal pressures cannot realize what they mean. For a brief space I have endured about a quarter of the pressure to which the *Clyde* was then subjected, and although the pressure was increased for me scientifically it was most agonizing and felt as though my skull were being held in a vice that was being screwed inexorably inwards. This agony lasted just as long as it took me to equalize the pressure inside my body with the external pressure and then the danger and the pain passed away simultaneously.

The lives of all on board the *Clyde* depended upon the honest work of the men who built her. If the men in the shipyards had scamped their work, if they had not done their best, there was nothing to prevent the sea from doing its worst. The pressure squeezed down on the hull, feeling cunningly for some weakness, for a few faulty rivets by which the forces of death and destruction could gain entry.

Loud noises issued from the metal which groaned as if in pain. The startled eyes of the men watched a four-inch solid pillar start to bend as the weight of the sea pressed down on the hull. One of the motors began to whine eerily as the pressure distorted the great starboard propeller shaft outside the ship and pinched it in one of the glands. The pressure actually bent the shaft. To prevent fire and damage, the motor was immediately switched off. The whole stern of the *Clyde* was distorted by the pressure. Pillar after pillar built into her to enable her to sustain such an ordeal bent to a greater or lesser degree, even solid pillars up to five inches in diameter. But in that crisis the fine work of the shipwrights triumphed and saved the *Clyde* and her crew.

No sooner did Lieutenant F. E. Macvie stop her downward dive than he started to blow some of the ballast from her main tanks aft in order to bring her stern up into a safer depth, after which he expelled the surplus weights from the other tanks until he managed to trim the ship and bring her under control again.

By this time a pattern of eight depth charges rained down into the sea. Fortunately the enemy was off the mark, although the last explosion broke some of the lamps, and fractured one of the oil pipes. For ten minutes the hydrophone operator heard the sound of ships nearby, then the sounds faded, and the *Clyde* moved up to a safer depth and stole out to sea.

A further attack was made by the Fleet Air Arm and the Coastal Command in which the *Scharnhorst* sustained further damage from direct hits by bombs on the stern and near the turrets, damage which put her out of action for months.

Not in vain did the *Clyde* watch and wait off the Norwegian coast. In very bad weather her captain struck and scored a hit which made the *Scharnhorst* vulnerable to the British air attack. It was a shrewd blow and a fine success. As the captain of his flotilla remarked: "I consider this to have been a finely executed attack under most difficult conditions."

Not that Lieutenant-Commander Ingram was inclined to accept all the credit for himself. None knew better than he how difficult it was to keep the *Clyde* below the surface and how one glimpse of her would have foiled his attack. His sense of fairplay was such that he very generously gave Lieutenant Macvie much of the credit for his successful encounter.

Few men would have envied him on his next

patrol, for the Norwegian seas seemed determined to exact vengeance upon the *Clyde* for her previous escape. A terrific gale blew up on July 12, 1940, and raged unabated for three days. The captain kept the *Clyde* under as much as possible to avoid the force of the waves. But he was obliged to surface every night to recharge the batteries and this gave the seas the chance to do their worst. The result was that she came out of that gale badly shaken up. Her main aerial was carried away, some defects developed in the hull under the hammer blows of the sea, and the gun shield which was designed to withstand the impact of enemy shells was unable to stand the impact of the great seas which badly buckled it and damaged the gun gear and platform. Despite the fact that his foreplanes were rendered useless by the seas and his gun knocked out of action, he would not think of returning to base, but calmly continued to search for the enemy until the time came to return home.

Not often does a submarine commander thank *God* that his attack was unsuccessful, yet the captain of the *Clyde* did so during another patrol. Led by his orders to expect a U-boat in his area, he was not surprised to sight a conning-tower in the moonbeams that night and attacked with torpedoes as soon as he could. Owing to the conditions and tactics of the other submarine, he missed the target.

The fates were kind to him. A few minutes later a signal from the *Truant* told him she was in his area. At that time the *Truant* ought to have been nearly a hundred miles distant on her way home, but unforeseen circumstances had slowed down her passage and laid her open to this unexpected attack. Thus the Royal Navy was saved from a tragic disaster.

On another occasion the *Clyde* was forced to go even deeper than she went in her plunge off Norway. For the second time in less than a year the relentless pressure of the sea caught her in its grip and strove to crush her. The astounded eyes of the engineer watched the supporting pillars bow and bend under the strain. The powerful hull of the ship was pressed in for two and a half inches. The engines were forced outward at the tops with the result that the propeller shafts were pinched in the glands which took them through the engine-room bulkhead and the packing caught fire owing to the friction. Several pipes were fractured by the distortion which ensued. But the work of man's hands stood the strain and the *Clyde* survived.

Directly she was trimmed and steered a hundred feet nearer the surface, the propeller shafts ran true again and the bent pillar supports automatically sprang back into their original positions as the pressure on them relaxed. It was a remarkable demonstration, not only of the pressure of the sea, but also of the strength of the handiwork of the British shipbuilders.

18

ATTACKS AND ESCAPES

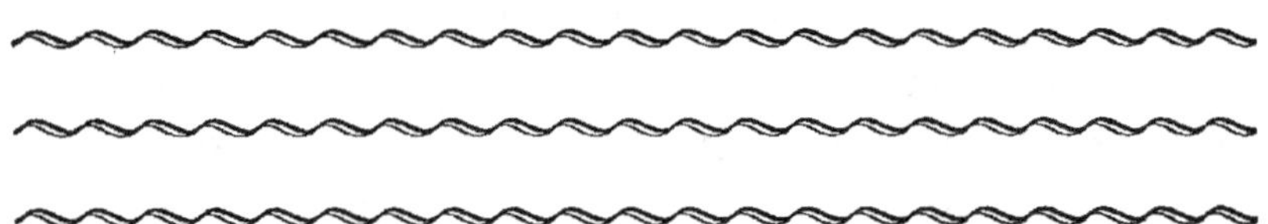

ONE day we may learn about the cargo of a steamer of 7,000 tons which was seen through the periscope of the *L27* about 3 o'clock on the afternoon of October 15, 1940, off the French coast near Cape Barfleur; but until we have vanquished the Germans and can examine their records we are thrown back upon conjecture. One thing is certain: the cargo must have been extremely valuable—a fact which the Germans proved by giving the steamer an escort of 7 trawlers, each carefully camouflaged. The big escort shows how badly the enemy wanted that cargo, and although we do not know what it was, we have the satisfaction of knowing that it never reached them.

It must have been galling to the Nazis when she was sunk; but what the German naval staff would have said if they had know that their precious ship was sunk by an old training submarine of the British Navy is something we must leave to the imagination.

Yet the *L27* was merely a training submarine which only the dire necessity of the times compelled the Admiralty to send out on a war patrol. On October 14th her captain, Lieutenant R. E. Campbell, saw that the Germans were carefully sweeping the approaches to Cherbourg to make sure that the channel was clear of mines—generally a sign of a ship making for port. He was, therefore, prepared to see this steamer next day, although the escort was much more spectacular than he had anticipated. The seven trawlers were steaming in a great half-circle in front of the steamer, so disposed as to make an attack almost —but not quite—impossible.

For half an hour Lieutenant Campbell manœuvred the *L27* to get within striking distance of the steamer, which was steaming at 15 knots, and at 3:35 p.m. he fired three torpedoes, all of which hit the target.

At once the hydrophone effect from the engines of the steamer ceased, to prove that she had been destroyed. Some broken lights in the submarine as she went down to avoid the counter-attack testified to the force of the explosion. The captain of the *L27* had just six minutes to wait before the enemy started to attack him and then in the next sixteen minutes the enemy dropped eighteen charges. Although some were close, all missed the mark and after being hunted for six hours by trawlers and torpedo boats, the *L27* got clear. It was a fine piece of work.

Equally fine was the attack carried out by Lieutenant M. A. Langley in the *H29* on September 16, 1940.

A hint reached him just before midnight on September 15th that a convoy was on the move and he went off at full speed to try to intercept. By 4:30 on the morning of Septmber 16th his hydrophone operator reported strong hydrophone effect to port. For the last hour or two the moon, which had previously been obscured by cloud, had been shining brilliantly and it was possible to see through the periscope for a distance of eight miles. Conditions were so good that Lieutenant Langley made up his mind to make his attack when submerged. Just at this time, however, the clouds obscured the moon again and so reduced visibility that Lieutenant Langley changed his plan and decided to run the risk of attacking on the surface.

He surfaced until the bridge was just awash and within a minute sighted a big convoy about two miles distant. There were tankers and passenger steamers and merchantmen ranging from 12,000 tons down to 5,000 tons, and he exercised his skill during the next ten minutes in stealing closer until he was three-quarters of a mile away, when he fired torpedoes at a group of eight ships all bunched up together.

Diving immediately, he heard two torpedoes hit, but whether he torpedoed one or two ships it is impossible to say, as he was obliged to go to ground to reload his torpedo tubes, after which came the task of escaping from the hunting craft.

Although Lieutenant Langley conducted his attack

like a veteran, except for a short patrol in June and one or two other odd days he had not been able to train himself or his crew under war conditions. This is what made his success so outstanding, and won for him the D.S.C.

In the space available nothing like justice can be done to the actions of Commander Geoffrey M. Sladen, D.S.O. and Bar, D.S.C., whose fine work in the *Trident* from the North Cape to the Azores has won the admiration and respect of all submariners. His first patrol in May, 1940, led to an exciting chase of a German ship which he failed to torpedo and subsequently attack by gunfire until he drove her ashore to become a total loss.

"Realising that retribution would soon be upon me and wishing to be clear of restricted waters, I made a somewhat undignified exit to seaward at full speed," he said later.

The retribution took the form of nineteen depth charges, but he escaped without damage, although the *Trident* dived to a crushing depth and a chain of buckets had to be organized by the crew to bale out the engine-room bilges and pass the water forward to prevent the engines from flooding. He groped his way through the next patrol in a dense fog which blanketed him almost without intermission.

Several enemy ships fell to his torpedoes and gun in Norwegian waters, especially in the autumn of 1941, when he made slashing attacks on the German convoys conveying munitions to the Finnish and German troops besetting our allies in North Russia. Two of the ships he sank in these latter attacks were transports laden with troops, so the enemy must have suffered severely. His brilliant and daring surface attack on the *Prinz Eugen* off the coast of Norway after the German cruiser had escaped from Brest brought him a Bar to his D.S.O., but not until a later date will it be possible to deal at full length with these forays which helped to spread confusion among the enemy. In peaceful days Commander Sladen played for England on the rugby field; and he has since fought for her magnificently on and under the pitiless seas.

Notwithstanding that this book is devoted to the action and adventures of the submarines of the Royal Navy, it would seem fitting to place on record a brief account of the escape of the Polish submarine *Orzel* from the Baltic in the early days of the war, about which much has already been written. Leaving the port of Gdynia on September 1, 1941, the *Orzel* patrolled in the vicinity for four days before moving off into the Baltic where she patrolled for a further nine days, during which time there was trouble with the air compressors, and the command largely devolved upon Lieutenant Andrew Piasecki, owing to the sickness of the captain. The feelings of the crew of the *Orzel* as they patrolled in the Baltic while Poland was being raped and murdered can be imagined, but no thought of surrender clouded their minds.

Putting into Tallinn for repairs, the *Orzel* after a

lapse of twenty-four hours, was interned by the authorities who seized her charts, her small arms, the breeches of her guns and some of her torpedoes as well as her ammunition. After drawing her teeth, an armed guard was placed on board to make sure that she did not escape.

But Lieutenant Piasecki promptly took command of the *Orzel* and under his inspiring leadership a plan of escape was formulated. He was bent on breaking out before his remaining torpedoes were removed, so all but a few strands of the mooring wires were cut from inside the submarine. On the night of September 17-18th one of the crew crept ashore and severed the cable of the floodlights on the jetty, and as soon as the lights went out, the armed guards on the jetty were dealt with. Then the *Orzel's* motors were started and she broke away from the quay and made for the harbour entrance, carrying the two guards on board as prisoners. Grounding on the harbour bar, she had to blow her tanks to get off, while the guns ashore and from the ships were trying to destroy her. Neither shells nor depth charges could stop the *Orzel*, and Lieutenant Piasecki escaped into the Baltic.

By October 8th the shortage of drinking water made it imperative for them to break out of the Baltic, and Lieutenant Piasecki succeeded in making his way through the maze of shoals and islands without a chart. All that he had to help him to accomplish this fine feat of navigation was a list of lights, and when he reached the Skaw he put his prisoners ashore, after holding them for five days.

The proud Poles were determined to create a good impression when they arrived in Britain and to appear as worthy representatives of their beloved Poland, so they devoted some time to cleaning ship and washing and shaving themselves before they reached their Scottish rendezvous, to thrill the world with their remarkable escape. To-day the *Orzel* lies in an unknown grave, but her spirit survives in the crews who man the other submarines of the Polish navy.

Less well known than the *Orzel*, the *Wilk* was the first submarine of the Polish navy to make her escape from the Baltic to Great Britain after adventures that were equally thrilling. In those days the Germans boasted to the world that they had sunk twelve Polish submarines, whereas Poland possessed no more than five.

Day by day as the crew of the *Wilk* listened to the wireless news of what was happening in Poland and France they became more and more excited and wondered what they should do. "We can either remain in the Baltic as long as possible or try to get to Britain," said their captain, Lieutenant-Commander B. Krawczyk.

His first officer who is now Lieutenant-Commander B. S. Romanowski was intent on reaching England. The crew were willing and anxious to make the attempt. They had no doubt about the risks. The Sound was announced as being mined on both sides. The lights by which they could find their way in normal times through the intricate channels were extinguished, the German destroyers were seeking to kill them, but they were determined to run the gauntlet even if they died in the attempt.

For three days they lay watching the shipping traffic to try to discover a safe passage through the Sound to the Kattegat; they saw the merchantmen drop anchor in daylight close to the Swedish coat and form convoys after nightfall to go through the channel. On the third night the captain of the *Wilk* brought her to the surface to let a convoy guide him through.

In and out the convoy zigzagged, with the *Wilk* carefully following their every movement at a distance. They were in the narrowest part of the passage when the look-outs on the submarine sighted two German destroyers approaching. The Poles had made up their minds that they would never surrender to the Germans. The torpedo tubes were packed with high explosives to blow up the boat in an emergency. Men were waiting to open the Kingston valves to sink her at the captain's order. The *Wilk* was in utter darkness. The crew were at their posts with lifebelts on, the gun's crew stood by ready to fight for their lives.

The channel was too narrow for the *Wilk* to turn in; all she could do was to go straight on toward the approaching German destroyers. In that crisis

Lieutenant-Commander Romanowski saw one of the crew smile happily as he took the butcher's knife from the galley. "If any Germans try to pick me up out of the water, I will show them!" he said grimly.

The German destroyers with unscreened lights approached the submarine. The crew of the *Wilk* waited like athletes listening for the starter's pistol. A broadside from the destroyers would have blown the *Wilk* out of the water. The Polish submarine and the German destroyers drew abreast, not more than sixty or seventy yards apart. No gun spoke. The destroyers held on their course. The *Wilk* slid past them.

Suddenly, as the distance between submarine and the destroyers opened out, the rear destroyer switched on a searchlight and focused it full upon the *Wilk*. The escaping submarine was discovered.

"Now they will return and give us hell," thought Romanowski.

Directly the channel opened out, the captain of the *Wilk* turned to wait for them. But they did not come. They proceeded steadily on their way.

The destroyer which sighted the *Wilk* mistook her for a Swedish submarine, and there was a furious scene when the German Naval Attaché discovered from the Swedish authorities that no Swedish submarine was in those waters at that time.

"It was a very big moment in our lives when we came to Britain," said Lieutenant-Commander Romanowski long afterwards, and the memory of that moment made his eyes grow dim. "We were heart-broken and very depressed. But when we came to our base there was the whole British Navy lined up cheering us. We saw the great fleet. Britain was fighting. It heartened us up immediately."

The *Wilk* was a mine-layer of about 1,000 tons manned by 5 officers and 42 men, and she laid more than one batch of "eggs" to bring discomfiture to her enemies. Once when the enemy disturbed her and put her to ground, the hunt lasted from 5 o'clock in the morning until 10 o'clock at night, during which time ninety-seven depth charges were dropped. The crew never worried about depth charges after that.

The cool courage of the Polish submariners matches that of the men of the Royal Navy.

One morning in 1940 Lieutenant-Commander Romanowski was on the bridge when he detected a slight blur in the fog and at once changed course. He could see nothing except a white wake approaching very quickly. The signalman pointed and gasped.

There was a big jolt. The *Wilk* stopped in her course. Her stern seemed to lift right out of the water. Lights were smashed. Ratings were thrown out of their bunks. Then she shivered and vibrated as she plunged forward again.

She had collided with a U-boat which stripped three of the blades from her port propeller and one from her starboard propeller, bending one and leaving two intact. The mine compartment started to leak. Other leaks appeared and before the leaks could be located there were ten tons of water in the engine-room.

As for the exterior damage, no one knew what had happened. When the port propeller was started it made the *Wilk* vibrate so badly that it had to be stopped. The starboard propeller was a little better, but it began to make the boat vibrate unduly if run at more than about five knots.

Despite the damage, the captain determined to continue his patrol and next day went off to try to intercept an enemy ship. Settling on the bottom in about 200 feet of water, he listened for the enemy. The leaks opened under the pressure. With pumps unable to keep the water down, it was only with difficulty that the captain managed to lighten the *Wilk* sufficiently to bring her to the surface.

Still the captain would not give up. The *Wilk* was leaking. She dared not dive without endangering her safety. She could only make five knots on the surface, yet the captain persisted in remaining on patrol for another day. Then he signalled for permission to leave his sector and aircraft and warships were sent out to escort the *Wilk* back to base.

These Polish submariners who are fighting so fearlessly to destroy Nazi tyranny are very gallant allies of the United Nations.

19

PATROLS OF THE *UTMOST*

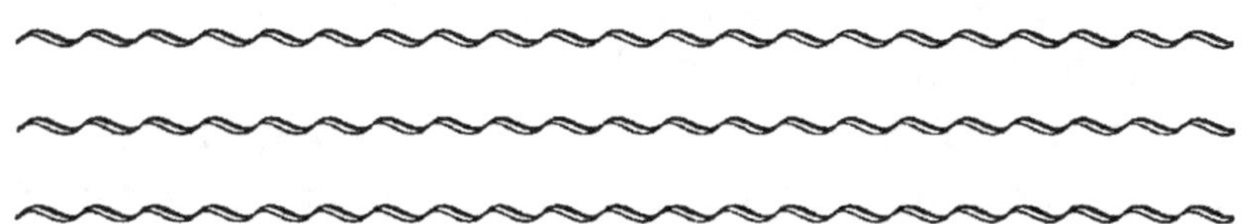

To SINK an enemy cruiser or battleship is the dream of every submarine captain, and among those to accomplish the feat is Lieutenant-Commander Richard Douglas Cayley, D.S.O. and Double Bar, whose courageous attacks in the Mediterranean during 1941 wrought havoc to the Axis convoys. His crowning success was vouchsafed to him in the last hours of November 21, 1941, when patrolling in the *Utmost* off Sicily near Messina. Earlier in the day, considerable patrol activity was seen from the periscope of the *Utmost*; this went to confirm the observations signalled to the captain that a British reconnaissance aircraft had sighted some cruisers and supply ships approaching Messina from the north.

Remaining at periscope depth throughout the day, the captain of the *Utmost* brought his boat to the surface just after 7 o'clock in the evening. So determined was he to intercept and attack the enemy force that he decided to postpone the important nightly task of recharging the batteries in order not to interfere with the hydrophone operator's listening watch which was so important on such a dark night. Handing over control to Lieutenant C. E. Oxborrow, the captain had his air mattress brought up to the bridge, where he was wont of sleep at night, and made himself comfortable to await eventualities.

About 9:30 there was the sound of an approaching aeroplane and a night fighter flew over the *Utmost* at a height of 300 feet. The aircraft had on its navigation lights, but evidently failed to see the darker blob of the *Utmost* against the dark sea, for it did not attack. A few minutes later it flew over again, still with its navigation lights burning, and once more it failed to see the *Utmost*. That an Italian fighter was out was a good augury, but even better was it that the British submarine should remain unseen by the pilot.

For another two hours the *Utmost* slid gently over the surface. At 11 o'clock the hydrophone operator made his first report.

Instantly Lieutenant-Commander Cayley was up on his feet with his binoculars to his eyes searching the sea to starboard. In a little while he sighted three Italian cruisers. They were steaming fairly fast, at a speed of twenty knots. Rapidly summing up the situation, he planned his attack. The night was very dark. Behind him lay some high land against which he judged it would be difficult to see him, so he began to move off at six knots to intercept the enemy. In ten minutes he reached a suitable firing position 1,500 yards off the track of the cruisers which were steaming in line ahead with three destroyers forming an arrow-head in front.

He stood watching for them to come on in the night sight, which had been set during the run in. The destroyers were sufficiently close to the leading cruiser to cause no inconvenience at all. Selecting the last cruiser as his target, the captain at 11.12 p.m. gave the order to fire a salvo of torpedoes.

"Torpedoes are running, sir," reported the hydrophone operator.

Lieutenant-Commander Cayley stared at his target which was only 1,500 yards away. There came a vivid flash as a torpedo struck just abaft the foremost funnel; he heard the boom of the explosion, watched a red glare rise up for over two hundred feet and spread out like a gigantic mushroom which remained for many seconds.

"Got one at last!" he exclaimed, while the whole crew were jubilant.

With the sea illuminated as if by daylight, the *Utmost* was lit in every detail, making her so plain to the escorting destroyers that her captain dived at once. The queer thing was that although the captain expected a fierce counter-attack immediately, the destroyers dropped only two depth charges. Then they raced back to the sinking cruiser and could be heard moving about that position, picking up survivors, while the other cruisers steamed off at high speed.

Just five minutes before midnight there were great rumbling and rending sounds as the bulkheads gave way and the cruiser broke up and foundered. For three quarters of an hour all was quiet. The *Utmost* moved stealthily away from the scene. Then the counter-attack started in real earnest and during the next two hours 84 depth charges were hurled in a desperate attempt to destroy the British submarine: fortunately none was very close and the *Utmost* escaped without damage.

Lieutenant-Commander Cayley was born at Ahmadnager in India on October 6, 1907. The son of General Cayley, he was educated at Clifton College, Bristol; and although he has proved himself to be a superb captain of submarines, he was in 1931 conscripted into this special service which he grew to like so much that he afterwards became a volunteer. He is well-built, 5 feet 8½ inches in height, good-looking, with grey eyes, straight black hair brushed well back and a friendly manner which ensures his popularity wherever he goes. He plays so expertly upon the mouth organ that he is known among his friends in the service as "Harmonica Dick" and many a time they have blessed him for entertaining them during the dull days of inaction in Malta.

It was in January, 1941, that he flew there from Alexandria in a Sunderland flying-boat to take over the command of the *Utmost* from Lieutenant J. H.

Eaden whose experiences in the *Spearfish* are described in another chapter. Lieutenant-Commander Cayley's first patrol in the *Utmost* was what is usually described as uneventful. But on his second patrol he came upon a convoy of three merchants ships with a destroyer escort about 9:30 on the morning of February 12th, and within twenty minutes of sighting them he had the satisfaction of hearing one of his torpedoes hit an 8,000-ton ship which he selected as his target. The next hour was not too pleasant. The destroyer kept rushing overhead, making a noise like an express train, and dropping depth charges all over the place. The crew counted twenty-five explosions in sixty minutes, after which the attack faded out and the *Utmost* withdrew from the area.

On another occasion the smoke of a convoy was sighted just after 11 o'clock, and Lieutenant-Commander Cayley saw that the three ships consisted of an armed merchant cruiser acting as escort to the other two vessels. His first choice was to sink the merchant cruiser, a vessel of 4,000 tons, armed with 4-inch guns, but funnily enough she came far too close for him to do so and zigzagged past the lurking British submarine at a distance of no more than 200 yards. As she passed, the captain of the *Utmost* turned his attention to the other ships which were about a mile away. Through the periscope he could see troops in one of them lolling against the guard-rails of the well-deck before he fired three torpedoes at her. Little more than a minute later came an explosion so heavy that, in the words of the captain, "the *Utmost* was lifted bodily in the sea and shaken from end to end." A few seconds later came another explosion, and when Lieutenant-Commander Cayley looked through the periscope just one minute afterwards the troopship had disappeared—blown to pieces by the torpedoes which must have detonated her cargo of ammunition. .

Later on the *Unique* sank another of the ships.

Toward the end of March the *Utmost* was on the way to Malta when her recall to base was cancelled by orders that sent her off to try to intercept six enemy transports. After thirty hours steaming her captain sighted the convoy at night in two lines ahead, with a destroyer zigzagging in front and a destroyer at the rear of each line. Waiting until the nearest destroyer was past, the captain of the *Utmost* turned to aim his salvo at what appeared to be an unbroken wall of ships, for the ships of the port wing overlapped the gaps between the ships of the starboard wing. The night was moonless and starlit, so clear that the convoy was first sighted when seven miles away. At 9:35 p. m. he fired his torpedoes, and dived at once to escape the counter-attack of the destroyers. Two torpedoes were heard to hit their targets which were estimated to be a transport of 12,000 tons and another of 6,000 tons. The explosions reached his ears just after the *Utmost* submerged.

To his surprise the destroyers made no attempt to attack him at all. They were apparently so busy picking up survivors that they had no time to attend to him—which was entirely satisfactory to the crew of the *Utmost*. The diversion of the *Utmost* during her passage back to Malta was a costly one to the Axis and very successful for Lieutenant-Commander Cayley whose score against the enemy continued to mount steadily.

In the latter half of June he started a patrol which promised more risk than usual, inasmuch as enemy mines were thought to lie right athwart his course. The danger left him undisturbed, and when he came to the dangerous area he kept a continuous look-out through the periscope. Before long he sighted a mine of a brownish colour just ahead and altered course sharply to avoid it. Another and another came into view, causing the *Utmost* to alter course erratically as she weaved her way through the deadly area.

At length the *Utmost* passed a mine so close that she nearly collided with it. The captain, staring into the periscope, wondered if he had gone mad. The mine moved and something suddenly pushed out of the side of it—it was the head of a Mediterranean terrapin!

"Well I'm damned!" exclaimed the captain. "They're not mines, they're turtles!"

The *Utmost* had got among a school of terrapins and had dodged about forty of them in an hour under the impression that they were mines.

"I fully understand the phrase 'mock turtle' now," said Cayley after that adventure.

He was hunting off the coast of north Sicily at noon on June 26, 1941, when he sighted a merchantman of 6,000 tons without any escort. The sun shone fiercely. The heat inside the submarine was such that some of the crew wore only shorts and sandals, some wore bathing slips, others had towels wrapped round their middles, while one or two discarded everything until the captain expressed his disapproval of the men casting off all their clothes.

Working into position, the captain fired two torpedoes at the enemy ship. Although he scored a hit, she merely took on a bit of a list and seemed disinclined to sink. After waiting awhile, he struck again with another torpedo and this time watched her slide under.

Once off North Africa he nearly ran into an enemy tug towing a target at which the Italian batteries were firing vigorously. He moved away from that hot spot with speed. Another time he was sent off to find a way through a heavily-mined channel which took a dozen hours to traverse. Making light of the risk, he went ahead, taking soundings regularly in order to chart his course. In the last war, the mining of deep waters was not considered feasible, but in this war the Italians have overcome some of the difficulties and have sown mines in waters more than 1,200 feet deep.

The most courageous man could not fail to feel the strain of going ahead for hour after hour, not knowing whether the next second would find his boat entangled in the mooring of a mine. Lieutenant-Commander Cayley admitted afterwards that he breathed a sigh of relief when he got through. There was, however, no indication of strain in the message he sent to base to signify his success.

The next night another British submarine followed the course of the *Utmost* and got through safely, while on the third night the *Upholder* in charge of Lieutenant-Commander Wanklyn, V.C., ran the gauntlet and joined them.

A brilliant piece of navigation on the part of Sub-Lieutenant Patrick Nicholas Joyce led the *Utmost* to the rescue of the crew of a Blenheim bomber which came down in the Mediterranean, where it was sighted by another Blenheim which for a time circled the position. The *Utmost*, which was just returning from exercises, was quickly victualled and sent off with a medical officer to try to locate the men who were adrift in their rubber dinghy. Other aircraft failed to find them; but the navigator of the first Blenheim which originally sighted the aircrew, although he had been out of sight of land for hours, took such accurate observations of the position that he was only a mile or two out, as Sub-Lieutenant Joyce discovered when he brought the *Utmost* to the spot.

The rescued airmen were without food or water, and as the *Utmost* drew nigh one of the shouted: "Are you British?"

They had reason for misgivings. The men on the

bridge of the submarine bore every resemblance to a gang of Fascist pirates. Lieutenant-Commander Cayley wore a green shirt; the first lieutenant was wearing a red shirt; the cable officer stood upon the casing wearing a black shirt, while the second coxswain was down on the casing without any shirt on at all, ready to dive in to help the men out of the dinghy.

The airmen, who were not anxious to fall into Italian hands as prisoners of war, were relieved to hear English voices hail them, and in a short while their ordeal was over.

Like several other submarine captains, Lieutenant-Commander Cayley when making an attack becomes so immersed that he gives a running commentary without knowing it. And if things go wrong, as they once did, his remarks are not exactly parliamentary. This was the day when he sighted three Italian cruisers preceded by an arrow-head formation of eight destroyers while a patrol of flying-boats circled overhead. The cruisers were steaming at twenty-eight knots in an oily calm which necessitated extraordinary care in using the periscope. Turning to take up his attacking position, the captain of the *Utmost* estimated that the nearest destroyer would pass about 500 yards away. To his intense chagrin, however, it altered course to pass right over the *Utmost's* bow. In the circumstances the British submarine increased depth, and by the time the captain had her under control again the cruisers were out of range.

On his final patrol in the Gulf of Taranto he won

another success by sinking an 8,000-ton steamer, which increased the number of ships he had torpedoed up to 9 with an aggregate of 70,000 tons. When he came up for a sight next morning he found the currents had carried him well out of position to a spot only ten miles from the harbour of Taranto. During the next night the hydrophone operator reported the sound of ships from the direction of Taranto and the captain sighted two cruisers with an escort of two destroyers. Although they were at long range, the captain decided to take the chance and fire his last torpedoes—they missed.

His ensuing remarks when three heavy ships of the Italian navy came out and passed right over the top of the *Utmost* while he had no torpedoes with which to attack them can be imagined. "I'm afraid I used rather strong language," he confessed afterwards.

On his way back to England he had just sighted the Bishop's Rock off Land's End and was looking forward to a well-earned leave when he was ordered back to patrol in the Bay of Biscay. By the time the *Utmost* returned to her base there was not a biscuit left on board and the oil in her tanks was extremely low.

His most treasured possession is the Jolly Roger which Captain "S" in charge of the flotilla at Alexandria presented to him when he sank his first ship. It is a typical black flag with the pirate's skull and crossbones upon it. And painted at one side are nine white lines to mark the nine ships he has torpedoed, while at the other side are numerous marks to represent certain other operations which cannot be revealed until the war is over.

It may not be generally known that when an officer wishes to grow a beard he must seek permission of the captain, who can make his own demands. One day Lieutenant Oxborrow requested the permission of his captain to grow a beard.

"All right," agreed Lieutenant-Commander Cayley. "But I demand a six-inch spade beard."

Lieutenant Oxborrow let his beard grow and forgot all about razors for many a long day. But when he arrived home at his base, he was rather dubious about what his wife would think and requested permission of his captain to shave.

"Certainly not. Your wife must see you first," ordered the captain, so the bearded submariner went home, prepared for the most adverse criticism about his beard. He was agreeably surprised to find that his wife preferred him with a beard, so he no longer worries about a shortage of razor blades.

Nothing could exceed the staunch comradeship that existed among the officers and men in the submarine flotilla at Malta. Their admiration of the way in which the Maltese stand up to the repeated air raids is equalled by the admiration of the Maltese for the gallant officers and crews of the submarines who after suffering and enduring all the rigours of bombing and depth-charging at sea in their campaigning against the Axis, come back to relax for a few days amid the daily raids on Malta.

One day Captain "S" remarked how nice it would be to see the happy and contented faces of some pigs in the submarine base. "We must have a pig farm," he said.

Accordingly Lieutenant-Commander Cayley went off with Lieutenant-Commander Collett to the other end of the island where they each purchased a couple of pink piglets from a farmer and carried them back in triumph under each arm to present to the captain. "Here you are, sir," they said. "Here is the nucleus of your pig farm."

The flotilla took those piglets to their hearts. They made styes in a stone stable, took a field and divided it up into pens by building stone walls, they laid on water and ran wire round the whole enclosure. They bought more pigs and still more, feeding them on the swill which they collected from the base, until their pig farm had grown to a herd of eighty pigs. As the pigs matured they were sold, fetching prices which would make the average pig farmer pink with envy, for a pig weighing 200 lbs. would sell for £18. Directly the initial cost of the pig farm, some £200, was repaid, the profits thereafter were devoted to various funds for sailors, but mainly for dependants of sailors who had been lost on war patrols.

Lieutenant-Commander Collett, D.S.C., who possessed what the country people call "green fingers" because of the way plants thrived under his care, was one of the prime movers in the scheme and his flair for pig-farming caused him to be known on the station as Farmer Collett. After going out to sink Axis ships, he would return to the unconquerable island of Malta to devote his attentions to the pig farm.

The pigs themselves, for all their seeming stupidity, were not quite so silly as they looked. Some of them had a well-developed social instinct and used to greet the return of the submariners with pleased grunts. One sow with her litter of seven piglets became known as Snow-white and the seven dwarfs. She used to love to amble along when the the submariners were having an aperitif on the verandah of the wardroom and join the party. Once she was rather thirsty, and as no one would serve her with a drink she decided to help herself. Seeing a bucket of water in the corner, where it was kept for fire-quenching purposes, she found her face was much too fat to get her snout inside to have a drink, so he worked her snout under the bottom of the bucket until she tipped it over—an action which not only provided her piglets with a drink, but also suggested that even pigs sometimes think.

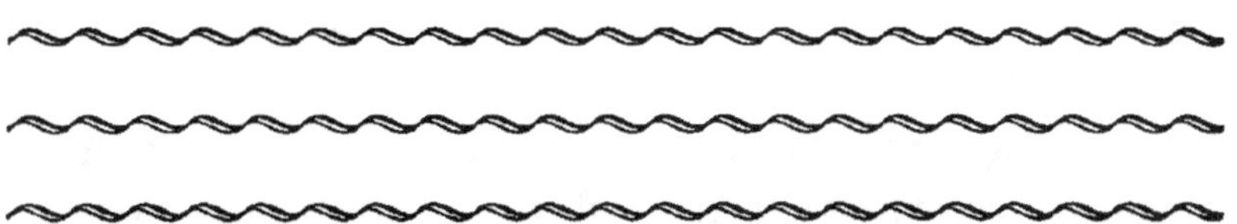

MEDITERRANEAN ADVENTURES

For an officer to receive the D.S.O. three times marks him out as a man of exceptional coolness and courage whose work has been outstanding. Yet Commander Ronald Hugh Dewhurst, D.S.O. and Double Bar, is as unobtrusive as the two tiny silver roses attached to the scrap of silk ribbon on his jacket. This Devon man who was born at the tiny village of Hemyock on October 10, 1905, had ancestors who followed the sea long before the days of Nelson when ships were things of beauty. With the imprint of Osborne and Dartmouth, he passed into the Royal Navy in 1922 and by the time he was a midshipman of twenty he volunteered for the submarine service on which his mind was set.

In April, 1940, the *Rorqual* left the China station, where Commander Dewhurst spent the first six months of the war, and made her way quietly to the Mediterranean which resounded to Mussolini's demands for Tunis, Corsica and Nice. The night that Mussolini declared war the *Dorqual* drew out of Malta with a full load of mines which Commander Dewhurst laid secretly and silently during the darkness in their appointed spot, leaving a considerable minefield to menace Italian shipping when day dawned. The operation was performed perfectly and from then on Commander Dewhurst was kept busy in the *Rorqual* laying minefields in the positions which observation indicated were most likely to trap the Axis ships. There is no need to specify where the minefields were laid; but it will suffice to say that Commander Dewhurst laid minefields in which a number of Axis ships came to grief. Altogether he is credited with having sunk by mine and torpedo about 70,000 tons of enemy shipping, a single fact which reveals why he was awarded the D.S.O. three times.

Like other submarine mine-layers, the *Rorqual* was equipped with guns and torpedoes. She was patrolling at periscope depth off the coast of North Africa one afternoon in August, 1940, when smoke was sighted on the horizon. The sea was a flat calm, there was not a cloud in the sky and the sun beat down fiercely while the men in the *Rorqual* sweated at their stations. Manipulating the periscope, the captain made out a convoy of two merchant ships escorted by a destroyer three miles ahead and determined to have a double shot at all three ships.

He must have known that he was trying to work something akin to a miracle in attempting to destroy the three ships at once, but that did not prevent him from trying, with the result that he sank the two merchantmen of 5,000 and 3,000 tons. The destroyer which he missed pounced down on him quickly, and shook the *Rorqual* with a well-aimed pattern of depth charges. But the submarine suffered no severe damage, and when Commander Dewhurst came up to periscope depth to inspect the scene, he found that the two merchant ships had sunk. By December, 1940, the ribbon of the D.S.O. appeared on his jacket.

Just before midnight on March 29, 1941, a tanker was sighted about two miles away, and the *Rorqual* went in pursuit upon the surface. The tanker, which later turned out to be the *Laura Corrado* of 4,000 tons, was seemingly unaware that she was being stalked, for the *Rorqual* was able by 1 o'clock on the early morning of March 30th to draw up to within 800 yards of her. Firing his torpedoes, Commander Dewhurst saw one hit in the engine-room and a huge flame leapt for 200 feet into the sky and lit up the submarine. Despite this, the tanker did not catch fire, so the gunners of the *Rorqual* put three shells into her below the water-line, and when Commander Dewhurst left her there was just a bit of her bow sticking up vertically above the surface.

Next day, on March 31st, the conditions were as unfavourable as they could be. The sky was deep blue, the sun glaring, and the sea like a mirror in which a ripple from the periscope would invite attention for a mile or two around. The *Rorqual* was keeping watch at periscope depth on Messina when an Italian U-boat was seen coming out of the harbour on the surface. Judging the course and speed of the enemy, Commander Dewhurst got away a salvo of torpedoes.

Half a minute later he raised the periscope and was just in time to see one torpedo hit the U-boat at the base of the conning-tower. As the smoke and flame of the explosion rose into the air, two other torpedoes struck the enemy aft and in eight seconds she was expunged from the face of the waters. Death struck down the Italians with terrifying swiftness before they had time to know what was happening.

Not until nearly two hours later did destroyers come out to hunt the *Rorqual*, by which time she was some miles away. She heard the engines of the destroyers fade in the distance as she continued to withdraw, and eventually she reached Malta safely.

The laying of mines, although so important, is not spectacular. But once Commander Dewhurst had the rare satisfaction of observing a ship steam right into a minefield which he had laid the previous day. He watched keenly at the periscope, waiting hopefully. A dull boom came to his ears as a big fountain of water rose from the side of a merchantman of 5,000 tons which settled and sank. It is rarely that the captain of a submarine mine-layer reaps a rich reward so quickly and can return to base to report such a definite success.

There was a day when he struck a fierce blow for the glory that was Greece by attacking a schooner and caique full of German troops in the Aegean after the Germans had overcome the Greek resistance. The gun's crew of the *Rorqual* soon ranged on their targets and sank both ships. Only the enemy knows how many Germans were drowned.

But the one experience which he has no desire to repeat was the failure of one of the exhaust valves which flooded the engine-room with twenty tons of water when he dived to 50 feet.

"Blow the tanks!" he ordered, and the *Rorqual* surfaced after being down about three minutes.

Thinking that it was only some trifle which prevented the valve from closing down on its seating, the captain dived again. But the valve still remained open and he was forced to blow the tanks once more to come up. For the third time he went down, believing that the valve would then close. But it would not operate, and this time the *Rorqual* was so heavy with the amount of water that had flooded into her that he was forced to use up all his compressed air before he could bring her to the surface.

Directly they were on top, they got to work to see what was stopping the valve and put it right. For twenty minutes they lay helpless on the surface within sight of land, for they dared not dive again with the faulty valve and without compressed air to blow the tanks. Eventually, after a most anxious time, the valve was cleared and the *Rorqual* was able to dive safely. But for the rest of the day the hunters were trying to find her and the depth charges could be heard exploding constantly.

"It was the most unpleasant experience of my life," Commander Dewhurst said when it was all over.

It was the Italian Navy which met with an unpleasant surprise on September 22, 1940, when Lieutenant-Commander J. R. G. Harvey sent the *Osiris* gently ahead in the Adriatic Sea which Mussolini boasted was closed to all but themselves. That the Axis did their best to close it is certain; but the questing British submarines found their way safely through the traps to strike the enemy when opportunity served—just as the captain of the *Osiris* planned to do about 5 o'clock that afternoon when a few masts peeped over the horizon. The sun shone, visibility was wonderful and there was not a breath of wind to stir a ripple on the water.

For an hour Lieutenant-Commander Harvey went ahead at periscope depth to close the range of the convoy which was revealed as a small tanker and two merchantmen of 2,000 tons each. Seeing that they were empty, he fired torpedoes at the destroyer before firing at a merchantman. A torpedo struck the destroyer as he dipped, and when he raised his periscope her bows were enveloped in a cloud of smoke. For two or three minutes a merchantman obscured his view, then came another bang, which may have been the boilers exploding, and five minutes later he saw the other ships launching boats to pick up the survivors of the sunken destroyer.

She was the *Palestra*, as the Italians admitted, and while the *Osiris* was entering Alexandria next day Lieutenant-Commander Harvey got a signal from Captain "S" that he was not to come in until he had received a special envelope and package marked "J.R." It turned out to be the Jolly Roger with the legendary skull and crossbones—the much-prized souvenir that marks the success of a British submarine commander in the Mediterranean. It is a banner of which these modern crusaders are as proud as were the Knights of Malta of their banners long ago.

Lieutenant-Commander Harvey, who also sank a 3,000-ton supply ship, was born in London on April 7, 1904. He speaks quietly, stands 5 feet 8 inches tall, is well-built with an open face, fresh complexion, brown eyes and chestnut hair. Going to Dartmouth at the end of the last war, he volunteered for service in submarines in 1926, and after doing good work in the Mediterranean in this war he came home to help to train the men for the new British submarine flotillas and pass on to them the tricks of submarine service.

Very different in appearance is Lieutenant-Commander Edward Dudley Norman, D.S.O., D.S.C., with his tall slender figure and studious face. True to naval tradition, he believes it is better to do things than to talk about them. "I had the finest crew a man ever commanded!" he will say, and mention with admiration the astounding courage of the Maltese whose heroic bearing under constant bombing is worthy of the Knights whose ancient excavations in the limestones have saved so many people from being wiped out. Those knights who fought for Christendom centuries ago have reached out of the past to help those who fight for Christendom to-day.

It is safe to say that there is one patrol in February, 1941, which Lieutenant-Commander Norman will never forget. The second night after leaving his base at Malta he sighted a tanker of 3,000 tons trying to run the gauntlet to replenish Axis oil supplies in North Africa. She proved to be the *Fanny Brunner*, and he crept to within 750 yards of her before firing two torpedoes. He saw one torpedo hit, watched the first burst of flame which quickly enveloped the whole ship. The burning oil poured out until the *Fanny Brunner* was floating in a sea of fire, a most awe-inspiring sight. It cast such a glare that he was forced to dive to avoid attracting the attention of other ships. But the tanker was not escorted, and he was able to give the crew a sight of her burning through the periscope. The biggest bonfire they had ever seen, she burned for an hour and a half before she sank.

A greater success came to Lieutenant-Commander Norman on the following night. The submarine was running on the surface when the officer of the watch sighted some ships about three miles away at 2.30

a.m. It was a starry night, with a thick black cloud obscuring part of the heavens, and the sea was smooth as oil. Through his binoculars the captain made out an Italian cruiser, the *Armanda Diaz*, steaming at seventeen knots with an escort of three destroyers.

She was but a thousand yards away when he gave the order to fire the torpedoes. As he turned off his tracks to go down, the officer in charge of the attack instruments, despite the fact that they were moving under helm, was able to give him the exact bearing on which the cruiser lay, and he raised the periscope just in time to see one of his torpedoes hit. With three destroyers almost on the top of him, it was unhealthy to remain, so he dived to the bottom and started to crawl away. For an hour the destroyers hung on and tried to blast him to bits, but they never came too close and eventually their attacks ceased.

By dawn, when the submarine was six miles from the scene of the attack, Lieutenant-Commander Norman raised the periscope to see what had happened. The *Armanda Diaz* was no longer afloat, but two destroyers were busy picking up survivors.

That was how Lieutenant-Commander Norman won his D.S.O., while his fine work in torpedoing a supply ship of 5,000 tons brought him the D.S.C.

On one patrol a member of the crew insisted on loosening the butterfly nuts of the torpedo tubes with a 7 lb. sledge hammer. The din he made was awful.

"You mustn't do that," said Norman. "Don't you

know there are thousands of ships listening all round us?"

He merely sought to intimidate the seaman into behaving sensibly and had no idea that there was a ship within a hundred miles. To his astonishment he heard the ominous chug, chug of an anti-submarine vessel approaching and he was under the tension of being hunted for over four hours before he escaped. To be trailed for hours by a ship that is listening for every movement and waiting an opportunity to destroy the submarine is not an experience which any man would deliberately court.

The hunt was barely over when the cause of the trouble came into the control room. He glanced at his captain, who was fatigued. "You're looking rather tired, sir," he said.

"You did that with your sledge," replied the captain. "I told you they were listening. We've been hunted for four and a half hours. You mustn't do it!"

"All right, sir. The next time I'll use a cotton-wool sledge," replied the culprit cheerfully.

Another member of that gallant band of British submarine captains who have made the crossing of the Mediterranean such a hazardous enterprise for Axis shipping is Commander Michael Gordon Rimington, D.S.O. and Bar. Born at Simla, in India, on May 21, 1904, the son of General Rimington of the Indian Army, he was brought to England in his infancy and from his earliest years was anxious to enter the Royal Navy, which he did after passing through Osborne and Dartmouth. The possibilities of an early command and the chances of independent action in a small ship drew his mind to the submarine service as a midshipman, and in May, 1938, he was captain of the *Parthian,* one of the big British ocean-going submarines which made the passage from the China Station to Alexandria just before Italy came into the war.

Apart from operations which it is not politic at present to describe, one of his earliest duties after Mussolini declared war was to carry out an offensive patrol of Tobruk which was at that time the main submarine base of the Italians in North Africa. Gradually he felt his way in, exploring the minefields and discovering the safe channels. He noted several merchantmen at a distance, a destroyer or two and a cruiser which he decided to attack. To his surprise he could see no indication that the port was netted against torpedo attack. Accordingly he worked into a position outside the harbour which gave him a good shot at the cruiser right through the harbour mouth. Imagine his annoyance when he saw his torpedoes explode just a thousand yards short of the cruiser— the Italians had fixed a net without leaving any surface indications.

It was over four hours before two destroyers left the harbour to hunt him out in Tobruk Bay, and then each took a half of the bay and careered about like express trains dropping depth charges indiscriminately. One passed right over the *Parthian* twice, while Commander Rimington listened on the spare headphones and explained what was happening. That was the crew's first experience of being attacked and they were quite unflurried.

Moving along the coast to investigate off Derna, Commander Rimington was lying down reading about 3 o'clock on the following afternoon when he heard the officer of the watch call "Captain in the control room."

Swinging out of his bunk, the captain joined his officer at the periscope. "I think I've seen a submarine on the starboard beam," said the officer.

Commander Rimington at length detected what appeared to be a little spike amid the seas. A further examination revealed a small Italian submarine bow on about three miles abeam of the *Parthian*, so, ordering the bow tubes to be prepared, Commander Rimington turned off his course to wait for the U-boat as she passed.

Keeping his periscope down for fear the enemy might see it and dive, he waited anxiously until he judged she was almost in position. A quick look disclosed an Italian submarine of the "Perla" class of 650 tons, with some ten men on her bridge and the Italian flag streaming out, moving into his sights at a speed of fourteen knots. In twenty seconds she was right in the field, and a salvo of torpedoes sped toward her—she was only 400 yards away.

For a little while the periscope dipped. Then the explosion shook the *Parthian*. The captain was just in time to see a torpedo hit right aft and a great cloud of smoke and water go up for two hundred feet. For a few seconds the bow of the U-boat, which had been blown right off, floated vertically, then it slid under and another scourge of the seas had met its doom.

"I looked round the patch of oil and could see nothing bigger than a matchbox," the captain of the *Parthian* said afterwards.

The nightly task of charging was often enlivened by the welcome sight of the aircraft of the Fleet Air Arm and the Royal Air Force raiding Derna and Tobruk. The men on the bridge of the *Parthian* heard the drone of the aircraft as they came over, saw the bombs explode, watched great fires begin to blaze in the velvety blackness as the silver fingers of the searchlights felt round the skies for the assailants and the flak criss-crossed in all directions to the booming of the guns. Such scenes spread a feeling of quiet content among the crew.

Commander Rimington was once attacked by an Italian U-boat when he was on the surface charging at night, and the sea was so phosphorescent that the bow of the *Parthian* created an arrow-head of fire which trailed away into a brilliant fiery wake that was visible for a great distance.

"It made me feel quite naked!" the captain remarked.

This phenomenon is caused by myriads of minute animalculæ, tiny sacs of globules of protoplasm that emit a light like a glow-worm, as was discovered by a French scientist in 1810. Off the coast of North Africa where the *Parthian* was then working the causative organism is named *Salpa Cristata* and the tiny globules join up into ribbons, coming up from the depths at night to float on the surface.

To suggest that the light emitted by these tiny organisms is sometimes powerful enough to blind the beholder may seem an over-statement, yet it is the simple truth, as Commander G. M. Sladen can testify, for one night just before Christmas, 1940, when in the neighbourhood of the Azores, his boat, the *Trident,* seemed to be passing through a sea of scintillating fire—caused in that area by the *Pyrosoma Antlanticum.* Later he wrote: "A night of astonishing phosphorescence so that it was necessary to shield one's eyes from the wash to prevent being blinded."

Twice on one patrol Commander Rimington followed the orthodox method of attack and was fooled by two steamers which continued to hug the coast instead of altering course to sea. Determined not to be fooled a third time, he made an unorthodox attack on a 6,000-ton steamer and scored two hits. For three hours the escorts kept dropping depth charges, and while listening to them he had the satisfaction of hearing the explosions and rending sounds of the steamer breaking up and sinking.

Probably his most exciting and successful attack took place in the Straits of Messina, where he lurked for some hours, just holding his own against the strong current. About 11 o'clock in the morning he saw an armed tug and three schooners pass inshore towing anti-submarine sweeps. An hour later he sighted a convoy of a tanker of 10,000 tons and two merchant ships of 5,000 and 6,000 tons escorted by a new type of sloop. The escort was zig-zagging at about fifteen knots, while the other ships proceeded on a steady course at ten knots. The 6,000-ton ship, which he decided to attack first, had the most grotesque camouflage he had ever seen and the Italians had even worked the pattern made by the deck cargo into their design. It was clever, but it did not save the ship, at which he fired when she was 2,000 yards away.

His other torpedoes were destined for the tanker which was due to come on in his sights about one minute later. The escort, sighting the torpedo tracks, turned down them to hunt the *Parthian*, while Commander Rimington stood there watching her rushing down on him and waiting for the tanker to reach the firing position. The tanker seemed to stand still while the escort flew—it was rather nerve-racking, by no means improved by the submarine dipping the periscope and blinding him for a couple of seconds. At the critical moment the periscope began to dip again and he was obliged to fire a little earlier in order to avoid firing blind.

As he dived at full speed to escape the escort, he heard his torpedoes hitting the merchantman. But he had left it rather late to get away, and he had barely got down to fifty feet and heard his first torpedo hit the tanker when his hydroplanes became jammed as the first depth charge shook the whole boat. While the *Parthian* dived steeply, a series of depth charges exploded above her down the port side. The shocks from the exploding depth charges made the crew cling to anything they could lay hold of. In the control room the coxswain was obliged to stand up and hang on grimly to his wheel; and the captain who was about to collect the headphones to hear what the escort was doing was flung heavily to and fro before he brought up against the periscope.

It happened that the galley table was laid for the crew's lunch. "All the crockery went for six!" said the captain when he got back to base.

Just as he managed to trim her at depth a pattern of ten charges exploded well above him. They made a big noise, but did no damage.

That was the most thrilling time experienced by Commander Rimington during his Mediterranean patrols. Luckily the escort vessel turned back to the tanker and gave him a chance of stealing out to sea. But he was hunted for six or seven hours by a fleet of motor boats before he managed to get clear and recharge his depleted batteries. After the attack the port propeller set up a fearful noise owing to the shaft being thrown out of alignment, and it was necessary to put her into dry dock when she returned; but otherwise she suffered no harm.

While there is nothing very unusual in an aircraft

sinking a submarine, it is a notable feat for a submarine to sink an aircraft, as the Lewis gun crew of the *Upright* did one day in Malta Harbour. Seamen F. C. Woolley and C. A. B. Sprott were on duty on the bridge of the submarine when they saw a Messerschmitt 109F chasing a Maryland bomber. With all his attention concentrated on his quarry, the German pilot failed to notice that his course would bring him within range of the *Upright*, with the result that the British gunners got in a burst which sent the Messerschmitt down smoking into the sea.

Lieutenant John Wraith, D.S.O., D.S.C., led the keen crew of the *Upright* on many patrols which cost the enemy four transports, a destroyer and an Italian cruiser. But his great triumph, and one which remains unique, was the sinking of a floating dock off Cape del Armi, about a mile from the Italian coast. Two tugs were towing the dock, which the Italians so badly needed, while three destroyers circled round to ward off attacks by submarines. With this strong escort further strengthened by two aircraft which flew overhead to keep watch on the seas around, the chances of a successful attack seemed negligible. The water was like a mill-pond. The watchful pilots could hardly fail to observe a shadowy submarine beneath the surface or the feather of the raised periscope. Yet despite the powerful escort and adverse conditions Lieutenant Wraith worked into position and fired a salvo at the dock.

As may be expected, he was deprived of the thrill

of seeing his torpedoes strike home and sink the dock: that sight fell to another British submarine in the same area, while the captain of the *Upright* dived for his life. More than once it has been pointed out what difficulties may be created by layers of fresh water in the sea, and at this critical juncture the menace was brought right home to Lieutenant Wraith. "We dived deep immediately, but unluckily struck a patch of fresh water and went down and down, well below the dangerous depths marks on the gauges," he stated afterwards.

Fortunately the *Upright* stood the strain and the captain crept away to base to report the destruction of the floating dock.

The other good work that he and his fellow captains of the submarine flotillas have performed to counter Rommel and protect that Artery of Empire, the Suez Canal, cannot be disclosed until the enemy is crushed.

GENERAL CLARK'S SUBMARINE

ADVENTURE

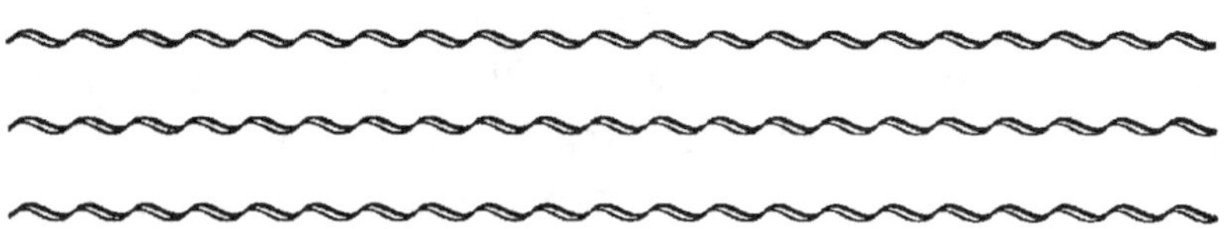

FEW missions have been fraught with such vast issues as the recent mission to North Africa to prepare the way for the Allied landing, and few have been so touched with drama. It was a mission in which officers of the American Army and Navy co-operated with British Commando officers and relied upon a submarine of the Royal Navy to land them at the appointed spot, and the courage and efficiency with which they all worked together has made history.

The leader of this hazardous enterprise, Major-General M. W. Clark, was the youngest general in the United States Army and was promoted to Lieutenant-General and made Deputy-Commander to General Eisenhower, who commands the Allied armies in North Africa. He was accompanied by Brigadier-General Lemnitzer, Colonel Holmes and

Colonel Hamblen of the United States Army and Captain Jerauld Wright of the United States Navy. The British Commando officers were led by a Yorkshireman, Captain G. B. Courtney, who was assisted by Captain R. P. Livingston and Lieutenant J. P. Foote, all three belonging to a Special Service Brigade attached to the Combined Operations Command under Vice-Admiral Lord Louis Mountbatten.

"About three weeks before the campaign opened it became evident that there was a large group of Frenchmen in North Africa anxious to co-operate with us," said General Eisenhower after the Allied landing was made and French help secured. "It was essential to send a staff of professional officers to contact and make use of these men and obtain essential military information."

"To get there," said Major-General Clark afterwards, "I used planes, trains, ships, submarines, canoes, automobiles—everything but mules," which was certainly a wide variety of transport. But the most important link in that chain was a British submarine in which Lieutenant N. L. A. Jewell carried the party to the lonely spot on the North African coast where they landed. It was a fine tribute to Lieutenant Jewell to be selected for this important work on the first occasion on which he had ever commanded a submarine on active operations, and the way he carried out his task justified the faith in his ability. The American officers, with full knowledge of where they were going, knew what they were going to do, but their secret was so guarded that neither the British Commando officers nor Lieutenant Jewell had the least idea of what was afoot.

From London the American and British officers made their separate ways by various routes and means to a certain Mediterranean port where the submarine of Lieutenant Jewell was lying. The danger of the written word involving a secret mission needs no stressing, and the first non-committal instructions which the British naval officer received were given to him verbally by the Captain of his flotilla. He was simply told to embark five American officers, who would be joined by three British officers, and then to proceed to a given point where his final instructions would be signalled to him at a certain time. As for Captain Courtney, when he left London he was merely instructed to join a submarine to do a special job that was so secret that he knew nothing about it at all. If his knowledge of Arabic and native customs suggested anything, at any rate he kept it to himself. Being a well-trained Commando, fighting-fit, he was prepared to undertake any task assigned to him and carry it through despite unknown risks.

The American officers went down to the harbour as darkness fell so as not to attract too much attention if any enemy agents happened to be spying around. They were met by Lieutenant Jewell, who led them down the conning-tower ladders and forward to their cramped quarters. Captain Courtney and his companions arrived and waited until nightfall before joining the submarine, in order to avoid inquisitive eyes. After all, it is not quite normal for seven army officers to board a submarine and steam away, and an enemy agent could not fail to be struck by this peculiarity and was bound to report it—which might lead the enemy to jump to conclusions. With so much depending on the mission, every risk that could be foreseen was guarded against.

"We were speculating as to the nature of the job when we saw, squeezing by the ends of our bunks in the submarine, Major-General Mark Wayne Clark, Brigadier-General Lemnitzer, Colonel Holmes and Colonel Hamblen of the United States Army and Captain Jerauld Wright of the United States Navy. As the submarine started to move out, General Clark called me into the wardroom and told me our job was to land the party on the Algerian coast, look after them during the day and get them back. I called my fellow Commando officers together and began laying plans," wrote Captain Courtney in his report, which puts on record the profound secrecy that veiled the mission.

While the British Commandos, who were the guides and guards of the American officers, were busy planning the best way to land and re-embark the Americans, Lieutenant Jewell remained in complete ignorance of what was about to transpire. Arriving at the appointed place, he signalled to base, and not till then was he informed of the task he had to perform—to proceed to a lonely spot on the Algerian coast and land the party.

The submarine reached the spot and Lieutenant Jewell and Captain Courtney, who realized that his knowledge of Arabic might prove very useful to the mission, saw the light appear in the window of a house. But dawn was already upon them and it was necessary to postpone the landing until the next night. All day the nameless submarine lay beneath the surface near the rendezvous while her captain and Captain Courtney studied the shore carefully through the periscope and noted various landmarks.

Stowed away on board were four collapsible canoes. These fragile craft made of battens and canvas each held two men, each were equipped with little oars, and in these canoes the members of the mission were prepared to risk their lives in getting ashore. The lack of space in the submarine made it no easy task to pass up the folded canoes to the submarine's deck in order to open them out and launch them. But the business had been practised, the difficulties were overcome and in the light of a full moon the first canoe was launched. To Captain Livingston fell the task of navigating the party ashore, and he and Colonel Holmes, who was deputed to make the first contact with the local people, successfully squeezed into the canoe and rowed to the beach. Four more officers negotiated the delicate operation of settling themselves down in their rather unstable canoes. But Captain Courtney was out of luck, for the canoe into which he stepped was swirled under the foreplanes of the submarine by a big swell that capsized it and tipped him into the sea before General Clark could get into it.

Scrambling up on the submarine, aided by the willing hands of those who were assisting to launch the canoes, Captain Courtney called back the last canoe and replaced Captain Wright by General Clark while the ratings were recovering and righting the capsized canoe. Then Captain Courtney and Captain Wright stowed themselves into the last canoe and managed by hard rowing to overtake the others before they landed.

Making their way to the house, they found that the owner had discreetly arranged for his wife and Arab servants to take a holiday for a few days, thus giving the Americans freedom to confer with the numerous French officers who had come to meet them. "The house," said General Clark, "was filled with French military officers in uniform, although they had come in civilian clothes." Feeling quite secure, the French officers donned the uniforms they loved and for hours these loyal Frenchmen who were risking their lives to save their country pored over their maps and conferred with the Americans who planned to help them to seize North Africa and deliver France from the German grip.

Of a sudden, about 7 o'clock in the evening, the breath of danger broke up the conference. The presence of the mission was betrayed. The suspicious

Arab servants, seeing so many strangers entering the house, told the local Vichy gendarmes that something strange was going on, with the result that two gendarmes determined to visit the place to find out for themselves. Fortunately a warning reached the owner of the house that they were on their way. Instantly there was a hubbub. Maps vanished with a flick of the hand. A French general shed his uniform with the celerity of a quick-change artist, and in a few moments was metamorphosed into an innocent civilian. Other French officers were just as slick. These men who loved France and were striving to save her did not wait for Laval's minions. They bolted through the windows and were lost.

The only hiding place in the house was an unlighted cellar encrusted with the dust and dirt of years. Pulling up a trap-door in the floor, the owner urged the English and American officers to go below. "The gendarmes are coming. You must hide here," he said.

Snatching up their papers and weapons, the officers dropped into the darkness, and the owner, closing the trap-door on them, scattered dust and dirt over it and piled upon it a heap of old tins to give the impression that it had lain undisturbed for years.

Waiting in the pitch darkness, the officers heard a banging on the gates. Then came the sound of excited French voices raised in altercation and the tramp of heavy feet overhead. At this critical moment the dust raised by the men as they went into the cellar affected Captain Courtney and brought on an uncontrollable desire to cough. He fought it back as long as possible and then the silence was shattered. Instantly somebody plugged a handkerchief into his mouth while another man slapped him between the shoulders.

In vain he tried to control the cough. Every moment they expected the trap-door to be flung up and a Vichy police officer call on them to come out and surrender. General Clark, who had 15,000 francs in his pocket and a carbine in his hand, admitted afterwards that he did not know, if the police came down, whether to shoot them or bribe them. The others, hearing him fumbling with the gun in the darkness, were afraid it might go off. "Put it away," they begged him.

Striving to suppress his cough, Captain Courtney heard the voice of General Clark in his ear. "Here, take this." Courtney felt something touch his mouth. It was a bit of chewing gum and it saved the day, for a few seconds after the Commando started to suck it, his cough stopped.

But the sound of the voices upstairs seemed interminable to the hiding men. For an hour and a half they lurked in the cellar, listening to the voluble French voices and wondering what was happening above. Then the voices ceased and after a short interval the owner of the house bade them come out and get away quickly.

They found when they got to the beach that a surf was running which made it dangerous to attempt to reach the submarine in their flimsy canoes, yet they were compelled to try, for there was no doubt that the gendarmes had merely gone to secure more help before conducting a further search.

All this time Lieutenant Jewell in his turn was anxious about the safety of the party ashore and wondering what had happened to them. At first he planned to remain submerged and keep periscope watch until the time came for the officers to return, but the rising seas made him alter his plan and come to the surface, for he foresaw that the changed conditions would create difficulties.

They did. An hour before midnight Captain Courtney signalled that they were in trouble and asked Lieutenant Jewell to bring the submarine as close as he could. Navigating his boat with the utmost care, Lieutenant Jewell brought her to within 800 yards of the beach. He did not dare to go in further, for there was only ten feet of water under his keel and an extra big wave might have bumped her on the bottom and jeopardized the security of the ship as well as the ultimate safety of the shore party, who alone knew the plans for overcoming the Vichy opposition in North Africa.

The first two officers to make the attempt to reach the submarine were General Clark and Captain Livingston. With the surf breaking round them, they got into the canoe, while the others coaxed the little craft through the breakers toward the open sea. Just when it seemed that the canoe was well afloat and would succeed in getting through, they saw its bow rise steeply on a big wave and a moment later it overturned and the officers were struggling in the water. Rushing to their assistance, their companions helped them ashore and retrieved the canoe—after which mishap they decided there was nothing to be done until the seas subsided. Meanwhile Lieutenant Jewell was very concerned not only about the safety of those ashore, but also about the safety of his boat, which lay in that shallow water for forty minutes before the signal of Captain Courtney sent him to seek a safer depth off shore.

Hiding the canoes in some bushes, the Allied Officers decided to pass the night close by, and posted sentries to keep guard. Even at that moment, with danger so close, the English sense of humour could not be suppressed, and Captain Courtney was tickled by the funny side of the situation, for he wrote in his report: "General Clark was soaking wet, so he borrowed General Lemnitzer's trousers. General Lemnitzer volunteered to do sentry duty, and borrowed Lieutenant Foote's trousers. Lieutenant Foote was junior and could not borrow anybody's trousers, but he was happy to make the sacrifice, particularly after having seen General Lemnitzer in all his dignity, doing sentry duty with a carbine over his knees—and nothing else."

About 4 o'clock in the morning a local friend stole

down to tell them that the police were going to raid the place in force and they must go at once if they wished to escape capture.

So they prepared for their second attempt to get away. Signalling to Lieutenant Jewell, Captain Courtney watched him cautiously and skilfully navigate the submarine until she was much closer than he thought it possible to bring her—with the seas still rough, their only chance of reaching her was to dump as much of their gear and arms as possible in order to lighten the canoes to give them greater free-board.

"Whatever you lose, don't lose the oars," counselled Captain Wright.

He fixed on the one essential for safety, and although they lost uniforms with thousands of pounds in their pockets, as well as weapons and other gear, they clung stubbornly to the oars.

Of all that party, Captain Wright was the only one to escape a ducking, and he boarded the submarine as immaculately as he had started out on his adventure. General Clark and Captain Wright ran the gauntlet first and by clever handling of the canoe managed to reach the submarine. For one dramatic moment, when General Lemnitzer and Lieutenant Foote were overturned in the surf, it looked as though the mission might have a tragic ending; but the seas swept them and their canoe ashore, and at their second attempt they got through. The other members of the party needed all their skill to prevent their canoes from overturning in the broken water, and no one was more thankful than Lieutenant Jewell when they got aboard and he was able to head the submarine out to sea and safety.

The margin by which the Members of the Mission escaped was so small that as she moved away, those on her deck watched two headlights draw up to the house and stop. It was learned, after the Allied landing, that they were in fact the headlights of the police cars arriving with the Vichy police to raid the place.

Had the Vichy police arrived an hour or two earlier, the Members of the Mission might have been captured and the landings in North Africa would have gone less smoothly and been marked by bloody losses. The work done by these American officers and British Commandos during their desperate enterprise cannot be over-estimated, for they opened doors in North Africa which would otherwise have been shut tightly against the Allies.

And a nameless British submarine under the command of Lieutenant N. L. A. Jewell made it all possible. The judgment with which he handled his boat during the delicate operations inshore and the skill with which he disembarked and re-embarked his passengers without loss of life were so highly appreciated that he was entrusted with the delicate operation of picking up General Giraud after his daring escape from France. For three days Lieutenant Jewell kept watch, then he saw a light wink and a little later a boat came alongside with General Giraud and one or two companions who boarded the submarine. While General Giraud was on board he recounted some of his adventures to the British naval officer, who in due course brought the General to a rendezvous where an American Liberator was waiting. Transferring to this, General Giraud was flown off to North Africa to assume command of the French troops.

Thus Lieutenant Jewell in his nameless submarine helped General Clark make history.